When Mourning Comes
Living Through Loss

Other Books by Chuck & Eileen Rife:

Marriage with an Attitude

WHEN MOURNING COMES

Living Through Loss

CHUCK & EILEEN RIFE

Essence
PUBLISHING

Belleville, Ontario, Canada

When Mourning Comes
Copyright © 2002, Chuck & Eileen Rife

All Rights Reserved. No part of this publication may be reproduced, stored in a retrieval system or transmitted in any form or by any means – electronic, mechanical, photocopy, recording or any other – except for brief quotations in printed reviews, without the prior permission of the author.

All Scripture quotations, unless otherwise specified, are taken from the *New American Standard Bible*, copyright © The Lockman Foundation 1960, 1962, 1963, 1968, 1971, 1972, 1973. All rights reserved.

Actual names of people in the stories are used by permission. Other names are fictitious.

Diligent effort has been made to track down the source of each quote included in these pages; if you find an error in the attributions, please notify the publisher or authors in writing so corrections can be made in future printings.

Note: To avoid pronoun awkwardness, we have used *he* to indicate he/she.

ISBN: 1-55306-373-2

Essence Publishing is a Christian Book Publisher dedicated to furthering the work of Christ through the written word. For more information, contact: 44 Moira Street West, Belleville, Ontario, Canada K8P 1S3.
Phone: 1-800-238-6376. Fax: (613) 962-3055.
E-mail: info@essencegroup.com
Internet: www.essencegroup.com

Printed in Canada
by
Essence PUBLISHING

To All Who Hurt

Table of Contents

Foreword 11
Preface: Why We Wrote This Book 13

I ❧ *Good Mourning*

1. Grief Exposed 19
   A Time to Mourn / Doing Your Grief Work / November 1981

2. Grief Makes Me Hungry 33
   Shutting Out the Pain / Addictions / Losing in Order to Gain

3. If Only, What If? But God!. 43
   Don't Dwell on the Future, But Hope in It / Embrace the Present

II ❧ *Building an Altar Out of Your Pain*

4. Memorial Stones to Wholeness. 51
   God's Trophy Case / A Living Sacrifice

III ❧ *Special Kinds of Losses*

5. Living With an Illness 59
   Jesus Understands / Dealing With the Pain, Loneliness, and Depression

6. Moving to a New City 73
   Gleanings from Genesis 12-20 / Questions to Ponder / Practical Advice

7. When Abuse Strikes: The Silent Grief 85
   Portrait of the Abuse Victim / Portrait of the Perpetrator / Lies the Victim Believes and the Truth She Needs to Embrace / Seeing Abuse as God Sees It / Help, Where Do I Turn? / A Letter From God to the Abuse Victim

8. Miscarriage: The Misunderstood Loss 97
   Misconceptions About Miscarriage / Reestablishing Your Life After a Miscarriage

9. Infertility: Empty Arms and Aching Hearts 111
   An Age-Old Problem / Equipped for Motherhood / Viewing Infertility as a Loss / Viewing Infertility as a Gift / Brett and Linda's Story

10. An Act of Terrorism 123
    Collective Grief / Redeeming the Time

IV ❧ When Death Comes Knocking

11. Losing Someone You Love 135
    Reflections on Death / Dealing With Death / Celebrating the Life, Sharing the Memories / Helping a Child Cope With Death

V ❧ When Someone Leaves

12. When a Child Leaves Home 161
    Saying Goodbye Doesn't Mean Forever / Strategies for Loving Detachment / Revitalizing Your Marriage in the Empty Nest Years / A Word to Parents of Wayward Children

13. When a Spouse Leaves 183
    Expectations Gone Amuck / Past and Present / Common Losses and Feelings / Developing a Support Network / Setting Boundaries / Guarding the Hearts of Your Children

VI ❧ Saying Goodbye to Youth

14. Growing Up and Out......................... 197
    Job Loss / The Death of a Dream

15. Growing Down and Out 205
    Self Preservation or Godly Preservation? / Adjusting to the Aging Process

VII ❧ Guiding Others Through the Night

16. The Church: God's Support Group.............. 213
    Complementing One Another in Our Differences / Seizing the Moment / Helping Others Grieve

17. Knowing God *IS* All the Difference.............. 221
    Our Foundation / The Greatest Loss

Notes 227
Reading and Resource List........................ 229

Foreword

I found myself grabbed by the stark realities Chuck and Eileen Rife address. Life's losses are faced and we are shown how we can win. I admired how with their and others' experience, Scriptures, and therapeutic insights, they sympathetically built a bridge from troubles to the very comfort offered by God.

I found myself not only curious about how to handle my own losses, but how to address the losses others experience. I found this book to be a useful tool in helping others.

No strangers to loss, Chuck and Eileen open their hearts and experience to you, dear reader. There is real comfort here.

If your loss is not covered specifically, the principles and Scriptures can easily be transferred to your situation.

Blessed be the God and Father of our Lord Jesus Christ, the Father of mercies and God of all comfort; who comforts us in all our affliction so that we may be able to comfort those who are in any affliction with the comfort with which we ourselves are comforted by God. For just as the sufferings of

Christ are ours in abundance, so also our comfort is abundant through Christ (2 Cor. 1:3-5).

Dave Peterson, ThM, LPC
President, Total Life Counseling

Preface

Why We Wrote This Book

Someone once said, "You are either in trouble, have been in trouble, or about to be in trouble." Life is brimming over with trouble. The Bible character Job, well-known for his multiple losses, said that "man born of woman is short of days and full of turmoil" (Job 14:1). Trouble and loss walk hand in hand. Yes, loss is an inevitable and continual part of life's journey.

You will confront some form of loss today. It may be as minor as a change of plans. Your husband calls and says he has to work late. He can't take you out for the special dinner date you had planned. It may be as major as the death of a loved one, a move to a new city, or the loss of a job.

Whatever the loss, it is crucial for our well-being that we give ourselves permission to grieve. We need to admit the reality of the loss, feel the pain triggered by the loss, and adjust to life without that person, place, or position.

Writing this book has been a constant venture of losing and gaining. At one point, through a thoughtless act, we wiped out the entire manuscript on the computer. We felt sick inside. We wanted to retrieve what had been lost, but could not. We ached for our loss, then adjusted our thinking. Perhaps we needed to approach the book from a different angle. This was painful to accept, but actually a blessing in disguise. With much consideration, we reformatted the work to include a broader range of loss issues. We found ourselves delving into the research process, which gave us a chance to refocus our energies, sort through ideas, and come up with a totally new outline for the book.

Werhner Von Braun once said, "Research is what I'm doing when I don't know what I'm doing." Thankfully, our research did eventually lead to an organized plan. Like working a puzzle, we experimented until we found the right piece. Sometimes this took hours, even days of sorting through a multitude of pieces. With much trial and error, we finally found the right fit.

When Mourning Comes represents the loss of a dream and the rekindling of a vision. Saying goodbye to one bus and hello to another. Weeping for a night, rejoicing in the morning. Losing… gaining… going back… moving forward.

We are no strangers to other forms of loss. We have grieved two miscarriages at four months gestation, a significant job loss, and a mother's death to Alzheimer's and cancer. We have watched close friends die and beloved children leave home. We have experienced multiple moves, several to entirely new cities in which we knew no one. In the course of this writing, we have been bombarded by loss on a personal level, as well as a national level, with the horrific attack on America, resulting in thousands dead, leaving our beloved nation reeling in grief.

You, too, have lost or you wouldn't have picked up this book. You hurt right now or know someone who is hurting. That's why we wrote this book—for us, and for you. We are each a part of humanity. Loss, no matter how great or how small, is a common thread that ties us all together.

Preface

We want to reach through the pages of this book and touch your hurting heart. Perhaps you will identify with one of the stories or glean comfort from a Scripture passage.

When Mourning Comes is a resource kit for those who hurt, which is all of us! Refer to its pages often as you walk through the seasons of life.

If this book helps you in any way, or you would like to share your thoughts on grief and loss issues, we'd love to hear from you. Please write us at: Total Life Counseling, Inc., 5401 Fallowater Lane, Suite C, Roanoke, VA, 24019, or email us at: *lifetimegrowth@juno.com.*

Partners for Successful Grieving,
Chuck & Eileen Rife

Part I

Good Mourning

Weeping may last for the night,
But a shout of joy comes in the morning.

~Psalm 30:5b~

Chapter One

Grief Exposed

*Whatever your loss, bring it out of the
darkness and into the light, where
true healing can begin.*
~Blaise Pascal, philosopher and mathematician~

*I*f you have lived very long at all, you have experienced some kind of loss. The moment you exit the warm, dark environs of your mother's womb and enter the cold, bright, noisy sea of humanity, you are forced to say goodbye to one world and hello to another. For a few hours in time, as you journey down your mother's birth canal, you agonize at the intrusion into your safe and peaceful haven. You are losing the only home you have ever known, to embark on a journey you know nothing about.

But it is time—time to stretch and grow into a brand new place with a parent's face you have never seen before. You have only heard that voice, but never seen that admiring face. A dark, sheltered space limited you from experiencing the next stage of development. Now, the painfully slow journey is opening new doors of opportunity for you. You will never be the same again. You will keep changing, growing, reaching, struggling for the next step in life's journey, for *it is time*.

A Time to Mourn

Ecclesiastes 3 presents a panoramic view of our lifetime in one brief paragraph:

> *There is an appointed time for everything.*
> *And there is a time for every event under heaven—*
> *A time to give birth and a time to die;*
> *A time to plant and a time to uproot what is planted.*
> *A time to kill and a time to heal;*
> *A time to tear down and a time to build up.*
> *A time to weep and a time to laugh;*
> **A time to mourn** *and a time to dance.*
> *A time to throw stones and a time to gather stones;*
> *A time to embrace and a time to shun embracing.*
> *A time to search and a time to give up as lost;*
> *A time to keep and a time to throw away.*
> *A time to tear apart and a time to sew together;*
> *A time to be silent and a time to speak.*
> *A time to love and a time to hate;*
> *A time for war and a time for peace*
> (Eccl. 3:1-8, emphasis added).

The word *event* in Ecclesiastes 3:1 actually translates as *delight*. Solomon exposes grief as a bittersweet experience, universal to all mankind, though it may reveal itself in different forms. Those who have encountered intense physical pain know what it is like to finally enjoy relief from that pain. The relief is all the better for having experienced the pain. So it is with emotional pain—the relief is so much better for having experienced the pain. The delight is more vivid and exhilarating in contrast to the agony.

Consider a barren couple who has suffered the pangs of infertility for many years. They finally conceive and give birth to a healthy child. Their joy is compounded, for they not only have a child, but they have also defeated their number one enemy—infertility. Compare that to a couple who conceives and gives birth easily. Yes, there is great joy, but the depth and intensity of the joy probably does not run quite as deep.

Our capacity to experience the depths of joy depends on our capacity to experience the depths of pain. Through the loss, our cups have been broken and emptied out. God stands waiting to mend and fill them with His overflowing joy.

When we expose our loss and pain to the light of God's truth, like colorful, multifaceted prisms, He shines through our lives in a multitude of ways, so that others, looking on, can see His brilliance. His light and energy is reflected through our lives. Why is this important anyway? Ecclesiastes 3:14 says that, "everything God does will remain forever; there is nothing to add to it and there is nothing to take from it, for God has so worked that men should fear [or stand in awe before] Him." Wow! When I present my life to God, the bad as well as the good, He takes that offering and makes something beautiful out of it, in order that those looking on will stand in wonder at God's marvelous work!

God wants each of us to have a personal relationship with Him. Nothing brings Him greater joy. He will go to any lengths to accomplish that purpose. In fact, He did, two-thousand years ago, when He chose to step out of the glorious comfort of heaven to enter the human race as a tiny babe. Even though the plan was conceived in the heart of the Holy Trinity, a shroud of sadness must have spread over heaven that day to see Jesus leave its gates. He grew up alongside of us. As the God-man walking in this fallen, sick and sinful world, He identified with us in our pain, loss, and suffering. He came to earth because sin, the root of all grief and loss, had separated us from God. God's justice and holiness demanded payment for that sin. God's love and mercy offered Jesus, His only begotten Son, to purchase our salvation from sin.

Jesus ultimately experienced the greatest agony anyone could endure—the cross—because He saw the joy that would come from His death—our reconciliation with God. For a brief moment in history, Jesus chose to endure hell in order that each of us could have an everlasting relationship with the heavenly Father. Even the natural elements cried out in mourning at the sight of the God-man—naked, abandoned, and abused—hanging on that old rugged cross. No price was too great to bring us to the Father.

Through the death of His Son, God exposed grief in all its gore and ugliness, and then He conquered it! Three days after His death, Jesus burst forth from the grave through the exertion of His own divine power! He became a living Savior! Over five hundred witnesses testified to the fact of His resurrection. Unlike any other religious leader, He actually rose from the dead and is now seated at the right hand of His Father in heaven. He is preparing a glorious place, beyond comprehension, for those who trust in His work on the cross for their salvation. He longs for the day when His children will be with Him at last. In the meantime, He gives His Spirit to all who believe in Him. He is our comfort, our joy, our peace, our helper, our counselor, our teacher. He leads us to the truth as given in God's Word. In His still, small voice, He comes to us in our pain and reminds us that this time of grief is only temporary. Someday, all tears will be wiped away forever as we enter the joy of heaven with our Savior!

Yes, Solomon reminds us that there is a *time to mourn*. It's okay to grieve the losses of life. Grief is vital to wholeness. But, Solomon also reminds us that there is a *time to dance*.

Our daughter plays a song on her violin entitled, "Tomorrow Shall Be My Dancing Day."[1] Written by William Sandy in 1833, eleven verses trace the life of Christ. Mr. Sandy tapped into the joy set before Jesus during His lonely journey on this earth. Through the words of the song, he offers the hurting heart hope in tomorrow. Healing takes time, but knowing that we will again dance, not just in the life to come, but here in this life, gives us hope that there are brighter days ahead. Each day of mourning brings us closer to the day of joy.

How long will I mourn, you may be asking? Grief responses are as varied as individuals, but there do seem to be some basic patterns. Let's take a look at a few.

Doing Your Grief Work

Loss can occur at anytime, at any place, and to any person. Loss is often beyond our control. Sometimes, loss occurs when we step out of God's will. In any case, we suffer not just from the primary loss issue, but also from secondary issues. Loss of identity, control, significance, respect, and loss of emotional, spiritual, psychological, physical, and social well-being are common threads that connect all losses. The unexpected death of a spouse can usher in feelings of helplessness. One may feel he no longer knows who he is, especially if his primary significance was centered in his mate. Worry over impending losses that may or may not occur can wreak physical havoc on one's health. Mid-life changes with loss of health, job, and youth can cause one to doubt his own worth and even question his spiritual foundations. No matter what the loss, certain grief reactions are sure to follow, and are a normal part of healing through the time of transition.

A person experiencing loss can expect to encounter various stages in the grieving process. Some stages will last longer than others. Some will overlap. What is important, is that the person allow himself time and freedom to grieve. The grieving process usually begins with **shock and denial**. The initial tragic blow is cushioned as the person adjusts to the reality of the loss. This period may last for a day or a few weeks, depending on the severity of the loss.

After the initial shock, a person may **express emotion**. Again, personalities vary. Some break down in tears the minute they hear bad news and later move into shock, while others remain frozen to the initial news and cry days or weeks later, after the flurry of people and funeral arrangements have died away. In either case, God created tears as a vent to our emotion. They serve as a refreshing cleanser for the body and promote healing.

Anger may then move in as the person reflects on the situation. He may be angry at his spouse for leaving him or angry at his boss for firing him. He may be angry at the doctor for misdiagnosing his illness or angry that he did not get a chance to fulfill a lifelong dream. He may even be angry at himself or at God. He may feel unwarranted guilt for the death of his child. He may think, *If only I had driven her to the ball game instead of letting her drive herself, the accident would not have happened.*

The blame game is easy to play during this stage. He may express his anger openly, lashing out at himself and others, or he may internalize his anger, leading to depression and despair. In desperation, he may "make a deal" with God, promising certain things if only God will restore the broken relationship, the job, or the unfulfilled dream. The longer the person harbors anger without appropriately dealing with it, the more possibility there is that he will begin to exhibit emotional and physical disorders. He must learn to manage this normal phase of anger in healthy ways.

Healthy grieving eventually moves beyond these early stages. The person is then able to accept the loss. He is able to talk honestly about his feelings with God and others. He admits his pain and makes the necessary adjustments to get on with his life without that person, place, or position. This takes time, usually anywhere from one to two years.

November 1981

Four months into my second pregnancy, I awoke on a Saturday morning with what felt like gas pains. I lumbered about the house all day, trying to take it easy. By 8:30 that evening, the gas pains were more severe. Chuck insisted I call the doctor. After dialing the number and enduring an endless number of rings, a doctor finally answered. I could tell by the voice that he was not my doctor.

Dr. Kramer said, "Can I help you?"

I nervously replied, "Yes… I am four months pregnant and I have been experiencing gas pains all day. I thought I'd better call and check it out."

Dr. Kramer barked back, "You're in labor, woman. Didn't you realize that?"

I was stunned. A few eternal seconds passed before I had the composure to answer. "No, sir," I finally managed to say. "I've never been in labor before at four months gestation."

"Well…" Dr. Kramer softened, "come to the hospital at once."

Nearly dropping the phone as I reached to cradle it in the receiver, Chuck came to my aid. "What did the doctor say?" he inquired. In shock, but resolute to do what I needed to do, I explained the situation. We packed a small suitcase and headed for the hospital.

The smell of antiseptic and the chill of the hospital emergency room further unnerved me. How cold, and sterile, and unfeeling, I pondered as I lay on the table waiting for the doctor to come in. Chuck tried to reassure me that all would be well, but I could see in his face that he doubted his own words.

"Mrs. Rife?" I heard the doctor question as the heavy steel door opened.

"Hi," I meekly responded.

"Let's see what's going on here," Dr. Kramer said as he methodically took his seat at the foot of the table. "Yeah, looks like you're in labor all right. You appear to be two centimeters dilated. Let's get you up to a room for the night and see if we can arrest those contractions. Maybe things will improve by morning," he said as he stood up to get the nurse.

Settled in my room, I finally had time to collect my thoughts. I kissed Chuck goodbye for the night and lay in the darkness staring at the empty wall in front of me. A small beam of light from the hallway crept through my cracked door and cast shadows on the wall. In my emotional state, I imagined happy baby faces dancing merrily on the wall, almost tormenting me, laughing at me. I still could not believe this nightmare was happening. I hoped I would wake up and find myself at home enjoying a normal pregnancy, happily planning for my baby's birth in five months.

The door to my room squeaked open and a heavyset nurse came to my bedside to check my vital signs and tuck me in for the night. As she sat on my bed, she offered words of solace. "You know, honey, this really is in God's hands. He will do what is best," she calmly stated. I knew in my mind that she was right, but my heart was too torn to accept the reality of her words. I felt so out of control.

Early the next morning, Chuck arrived back at the hospital to see how I was progressing. I actually felt better. The contractions were gone, and my hopes were revived that perhaps we would see this pregnancy through after all. Dr. Kramer came in to check me. Finding me greatly improved, he said I could leave in a couple of hours, with the instructions that I go straight to bed for awhile and see my regular obstetrician as soon as possible.

Awake most of the night, I now lapsed into a peaceful sleep. All would be well. My baby would be all right.

But that was not to be. An hour later, I was awakened by sharp pains. Sluggishly, I reached over to buzz the nurse. When she arrived in my room, she could tell by my pained expression that my condition had worsened. She immediately left to find the doctor. As it turned out, Dr. Kramer had left for the morning, probably to get some much needed rest after deliveries the night before.

Chuck silently held my hand as I rolled back and forth in pain. After what seemed like an eternity, a nurse and two orderlies came in with a gurney and proceeded to place me on it. By this time, I was in so much pain, I was begging God to make it stop. The swift flight to the delivery room was aborted at the doorway, as Dr. Kramer had not arrived yet. The orderlies left Chuck and I waiting in a small room right outside the delivery room door.

In agony, we waited and waited. At the time, I wondered why God would make me wait so long for the doctor to come. On reflection, I realize that in my pain, He was trying to speak to me. In an unexplainable way, I felt a measure of peace.

At last, the nurse and two orderlies came back. "The doctor's here. Let's get you into the delivery room," the nurse quietly said. The hush of death surrounded us, but I was in too much pain to fully absorb the reality of the moment.

Inside the delivery room, Dr. Kramer and the nurses busily worked, as Chuck tried to console me. After breaking my water, I felt a small object slide out. The physical pain lessened, but my emotional pain increased, as I realized our baby had been born.

I gathered my wits and questioned, "What is it?"

Dr. Kramer hesitated, but I persisted. "It's a boy," he answered.

"I want to see him," I calmly said. Dr. Kramer slowly walked to my side and stretched out his hand. Spanning the length of his hand was a perfectly formed, six-inch baby boy. I saw the tiny body, but knew my little son was in heaven with Jesus. I had to say goodbye.

As the orderlies wheeled me to the recovery room, I marveled to the nurse how anyone could purposely abort her baby. I had just observed a baby at four months gestation—a tiny, yet perfectly formed creation of God. I was already a strong pro-life advocate, but abortion made even less sense to me now. Emotional pain was beginning to replace physical pain as I entertained feelings of anger.

The next morning, I awoke to a nurse lifting the shades at my window. I felt nauseated as the blinding sun danced on my face. "You really ought to get up, honey, and get cleaned up. The doctor will be in soon to release you," she said in a matronly tone. I wanted to be polite and obey, but simply did not have the will to do so. I chose to remain quiet. Quietness matched the numbness I felt inside.

After the nurse left, I managed to get up and take a welcoming shower, but even the warm embrace of the water could not wash away the escalating emotional pain I experienced. Back in bed, I sat up and put on a little make-up in anticipation of Chuck's arrival. I wanted him to be encouraged that I was at least making some attempts to return to normal.

As I viewed my image in a hand mirror, another nurse entered the room and prepared to check my vital signs. Observing my wet hair, she chided, "Honey (always that word, which by now was beginning to sicken me), you really ought to be more careful. You don't want to catch a cold. You might give it to your baby." That was all it took. My anger crested and overflowed its bank. "I don't have a baby!" I lashed back. Ruffled, the nurse tried to maintain her composure. She quickly apologized, finished her work, and left my room.

By noon, I was checked out of the hospital. Chuck and I rode home, saying few words along the way. When we finally pulled up to our house, I looked out my window and viewed the long black steps rising up to our front door. The sight wearied me, reminding me of the arduous healing that lay before me. The very act of walking was a drudgery, but at last I managed to open the front door. Two-year-old Rachel was staying with a neighbor, so the house was morbidly still, as if sympathizing with our loss.

As I looked about the living room, I realized the house was just as we had left it two days before, with toys scattered about and a laundry basket full of clothes waiting to be folded. Peering into the kitchen, I observed the sink still full of dishes. Like a robot, I catatonically began straightening things up, picking right up where I had left off a few days before. Chuck encouraged me to rest and tried to hold me. I shooed him away, saying that I was fine, that I needed to stay busy.

I tried to pretend life was back to normal again. I wanted it to be, so why shouldn't it be? Neighbors came and went with covered dishes and expressions of sympathy. My mom and dad drove in from Tennessee to offer assistance, but I pushed them away. I even found it difficult to relate to my darling toddler, Rachel. She needed my reassurance and I needed hers, but I was in so much emotional pain, I could not respond. Perhaps I was afraid if I got too close to her, she would die too.

The physical indications that I had just been pregnant were blatantly obvious to me—swollen breasts with no relief from a suckling infant and a flattened belly once alive with a moving babe. I grieved inwardly, but remained silent around others. I appreciated their concern, but I just wanted to be alone. Some days, I just wanted to die.

Chuck did not even realize the depth of my depression, as I was adept at pretending around him. He did not seem to understand anyway, I inwardly rationalized. Yet, all the while, he too was grieving in his own way. He was concerned for my well-being, yet aware that I yearned for what I had lost and wanted to somehow regain my loss through another pregnancy. He grieved for my heartache, though as a man, could not fully relate to it.

By mid-January, I was fed up with my pain. One morning, after Chuck left for work and Rachel went to a neighbor's house to play, I took my Bible and fell to my knees in front of our large, upholstered rocking chair. It had been two months since our baby went to heaven, and I still inwardly longed to simply depart and be there with him.

I wept loudly and poured out my heart to God. I spoke to Him audibly and freely. "I am so angry, Lord—angry at Chuck for not feeling this with me the way I want him to; angry at myself for not knowing I was in labor and calling the doctor sooner; and… yes… Lord… even angry at You for allowing such a tragedy to happen in the first place. Why Lord? Why?"

There… I got it out—all the feelings I had been holding in for two months. I thought I could come home from the hospital and pick up where I left off, but in doing that, I denied myself the right, the necessity to grieve and thus heal. Only when I got honest before God about my true feelings could the real healing begin. From that moment on, I began to view things differently.

Our rocking chair sat by a double-wide window. The sun was streaming in through the pane (unusual for a winter day), warmly falling on me as I hunched over my Bible frantically searching for emotional relief. As I flipped through the pages, I came to Luke chapter one. Scanning the chapter, my eyes fell upon verses 78 and 79 which appeared to leap off the page in my direction. "Because of the tender mercy of our God, with which the Sunrise from on high will visit us, to shine upon those who sit in darkness and the shadow of death, to guide our feet into the way of peace." It was as though God had just written those words for me that very morning and floated them down through the sunlight. In His tender mercy, God had provided all the healing and peace I required through His precious Son (the Sunrise from on high). I was in emotional darkness, and He came to lift me out of my unending bleakness and set me on a path of wholeness and peace. When I finally determined to seek after God in the midst of my pain, He wholeheartedly responded and gave me the answer I needed—Himself!

My grief was exposed and it was time to mourn... to ask questions... to be angry... to cry... to talk... to write out feelings... to be confused... and then to do it all again. In some ways, even after twenty years, Chuck and I are still grieving. The intense pain has eased with time. The conviction that God had a specific plan in allowing our son's death has deepened with time. The realization that, for whatever reason, God wanted our son with Him in heaven and our other children with us here on earth for now, has been a stabilizing comfort.

Our griefs are never fully resolved until heaven when God will make all things clear. Every loss leaves a scar. What we do with those scars is the critical issue. Jesus suffered scars from the nails. They did not magically disappear when He rose from the grave. The scars in His hands, feet, and side remained to show the agony He had endured for us. Our scars remain as a constant reminder that we share in the fellowship of His sufferings, that we have experienced the depths of pain, in order that, ultimately, our joy might be made full. How? By the way God comes to us with His comfort; by the way He uses our afflictions to relate to other hurting people and offer comfort to them; by the way we learn to love those around us more actively; by the way we learn obedience to our God by the things we suffer; by the way He molds and shapes our character more like the Lord Jesus Christ, who endured hardship patiently; by the way He creates a hunger for heaven in our souls. If we enjoyed only the good things of life here on earth, we would never desire our true home where we really belong. Grief exposed, makes us hungry.

Chapter Two

Grief Makes Me Hungry

> Man searches in vain, but finds nothing to help him,
> other than to see an infinite emptiness
> that can only be filled by... God Himself.
> ~BLAISE PASCAL, PHILOSOPHER AND MATHEMATICIAN~

Driving home from a funeral with her son in the car, Jane lamented the tragic loss suffered by a family friend. Now widowed and left alone to rear three young children, Don was embarking on a long journey of grief and adjustment. Jane felt frustrated by the needless death of her friend. Such a waste! To see a godly family, truly desirous of doing God's will, torn apart and pierced to the very core of its being made no sense to her. She felt angry, tired, and, suddenly... physically hungry. She wanted to drown her sorrows with a hefty portion of food. Maybe the delectable delight of a big, juicy burger, crunchy fries, and a cool, crisp salad, followed by a yummy ice cream treat would temporarily abate the emotional pain she felt. She leaned over to her son in the front seat and sighed, "Grief makes me hungry."

The more I reflect on the grieving process, the more I affirm that grief does indeed make the mourner hungry—not always for food, but for other things as well. One person may lose his appetite completely, while another may use food as a source of comfort. Someone who chooses to divert his pain in unhealthy ways may turn to drugs to dull his overwhelming emotional trauma. He may jump into new relationships too quickly to fill the void that the missing person has created. Soothing his aching heart is the goal, so he may experiment with all kinds of temporal remedies to alleviate the pain.

Shutting Out the Pain

Someone experiencing extreme emotional pain as a result of a loss may employ different methods to defend himself against the deep hurt. He may **deny** the reality of the loss, refusing to talk about it or to cry. He pushes the pain further and further down within, pretending that he does not feel it. The tragedy of this form of escape is that, sooner or later, as one unresolved loss after another piles up, he eventually explodes under the pressure. Even Shakespeare encourages us to "give sorrow words. The grief that does not speak whispers the o'er-fraught heart and bids it break."

Another person may **rationalize** the intensity of the loss. To protect himself from the impact, he may say things like, "I didn't care for that job anyway," or "She's happy now in heaven."

Still another, may run from his hurt and disappointment by **idealizing** what was lost. Only the positive attributes of the person, job, or neighborhood are talked about. This is true even in the case of abusive parents. Often, children will shun the strong, negative behavior and only accept what was positive.

Sometimes, a person will **overreact** to guard himself against an impending loss situation. This is a common reaction for parents who observe their adolescent children forming more and more attachments outside of the home, and seeking independence from mom and dad. Feeling threatened, mom and dad may exhibit more control over their child's activities, at a time when they should be gradually loosening the reins.

Finally, a person running from his loss may use **regression** as a defense against the pain. Often, this is the case with young children. A three-year-old may be successfully potty trained before the death of a parent or sibling, but afterwards may have multiple "accidents."[1]

Any of the defense mechanisms mentioned above, are a natural tendency for the grieving person who is hungry for relief from his pain. However, if persisted in, they become a hindrance to growth and recovery. Ultimately, the loss must be faced and grieved if the person is to move on with his life.

If the hurting person fails to accept his loss and continues to seek inappropriate and unhealthy ways to alleviate his intense emotional hunger, he will remain stuck in unhealthy patterns and live a dysfunctional lifestyle. He may form any number of addictive behaviors.

Addictions

Addictions are addictive because they work. They do relieve pain, at least temporarily. Some people turn to alcohol, drugs, or even food to escape their pain. Others turn to unhealthy relationships, exhibited by codependent behavior, sexual addiction, or withdrawal from others. Still others, turn to activities such as gambling, stealing, lying, or excessive television viewing. Some bury themselves in work.

Addictive behavior is rooted in a love hunger for God. The grieving person has lost his connection with God, not because God has moved away, but because the person has tried to fill the void in his heart with substitutes for God.

Just stopping the behavior is not enough. The only way to remedy the addiction is to go back *through* the emotional pain. The hurting one must tell the truth about the loss and admit that he is hurting. He must allow himself to feel all the emotions related to his pain, such as anger, fear, rejection, abandonment, confusion, guilt, and disappointment. Each feeling should drive him to God for healing. It is only in Him that the grieving one can once again achieve balance and purpose in moving forward with life. He must be perfectly honest with God about how he feels. God will receive this honest interaction. He will not be offended or put out. He understands. Knowing that God is not angry at a person's feelings can be a freeing realization.

Feelings are neither bad nor good—they just are. Like physical pain, emotional pain is a signal that something within a person needs attention. If the hurting one turns to the ways of the world for relief, he will most likely succumb to three temptations: the lust of the flesh (sexual hunger), the lust of the eyes (material hunger), and the pride of life (power hunger), for all addictions are rooted in 1 John 2:16. These things will never satisfy, for the things of the world and its lusts are passing away, "but the one who does the will of God lives forever" (1 John 2:17).

The will of God for the hurting person is to admit the loss and confront the resulting pain in his heart. Instead of seeking relief from the world, one should focus his attention on God, who longs to satisfy those hungers with Himself. Sometimes, a person in pain turns from God because his grief screams so loud and so long, that it tunes out everything and everyone else. He curls up within himself and feels abandoned by God and others. He knocks on one door after another seeking a welcome haven from his pain. He may discover temporary entrance, but no lasting abode. This delights Satan, who is out for the person's destruction in whatever way he can accomplish it.

Just as physical pain should drive the sick one to the physician, so emotional pain should drive the hurting one to the Great Physician.

He is the God of all comfort. The person must keep seeking the Lord through His Word, prayer, and the fellowship of other believers until there is a breakthrough. Often, this will take time, depending on the severity of the loss.

I (Chuck) have found it beneficial to my own emotional healing, during times of loss, to write exactly how I am feeling in my journal. I try to be totally honest with God, just as David was in the Psalms. Then, I conclude my daily writing on a note of faith, jotting down some promise from God that I have gleaned from the Scripture.

Though I may not *feel* that anything about God is true at the moment, I exercise my faith muscles by declaring emphatically, in the face of Satan, that God is faithful. He is with me. He has a purpose in my loss. He loves me. He is my joy. He is my peace. He is working all things out for my ultimate good and for His glory. I declare these things to be so on the authority of the Word of God, feelings or no feelings. I put my will on the believing side, and eventually my feelings follow.

I usually have to repeat this exercise many times a day as my unruly emotions surge and overwhelm me. In order to do this, I practice biblical self-talk. I write out statements on a 3x5 card and post them around the house where I will be reminded of what God has done for me. When I pass these cards during the day, I stop and read them. I have even recorded these statements and listened to the cassette while driving to and from work.

For example, one statement might be, "I, Chuck Rife (you supply your name here), now thank God for His indwelling power." I make a list of as many of these statements as I can think of. You might try starting with ten. As you study the Scriptures, God will give you many more. The book of Ephesians is full of wonderful reminders of who we are as believers in Christ. With our identity firmly rooted in Christ, we can walk victoriously through the healing journey. We know that life's losses cannot alter our relationship with God, but rather deepen and enrich it.

One of God's divine purposes in pain is to drive us to Himself. Nothing else is quite as effective. In his book, *Through the Wilderness of Loneliness*, Tim Hansel, founder of Summit Expedition, writes, "A broken heart simply contains more room for love. In my own personal dark night of the soul, it felt like the vacuum within me was getting bigger and bigger. Then I realized that this 'hollowness' was simply creating more room and more appetite for God. My cup of emptiness became a Cup for His Presence and His Love."[2]

God is in the business of fashioning us after the likeness of His dear Son. Remember how Jesus learned obedience through the things that He suffered. Why should we frail, sinful humans think that it will be any different with us? Our stubborn, sin-sick hearts only learn obedience by the things we suffer. Lest we think this is cruel of our God, let's consider the payoff. If we hand our pain over to God, our suffering teaches us patience, opens up in us a greater capacity to receive and give love, develops within us a quiet confidence that God is Lord of all, creates a longing for heaven—our real home—and gives a deep yearning for God Himself, who is the satisfier of our souls. God desires that He be the center of our joy, for only He really can be. We will always be restless until we find our rest in Him and Him alone.

So, we lose in order to gain. If we become willing students of our pain, we will discover for ourselves that the gain outweighs the loss.

Losing in Order to Gain

The paradox of this principle is eloquently stated by Joni Eareckson Tada and Steven Estes in their book, *When God Weeps*:

> Gaining contentment does not mean losing sorrow or saying goodbye to discomfort. Contentment means sacrificing itchy cravings to gain a settled soul. You give up one thing for

another. It's hard. Hard, but sweet. You are "sorrowful, yet always rejoicing." You "have nothing, yet possess everything." 1 Timothy 6:6 (NIV) says, "Godliness with contentment is great gain" and the gain always comes through loss.[3]

Our deep hunger for relief should create within our souls a deep longing for God. In his severe affliction, Job said, "I have heard of You by the hearing of the ear; but now my eye sees You; therefore I retract, and I repent in dust and ashes" (Job 42:5-6). Job was familiar with God before his suffering, but pain opened the door to an intimate relationship with God as Job grappled with the gut-wrenching emotions, the questions, and the deep, repeated conversations with God. Suffering led to Job's humility and total abandonment to the will of God. He enjoyed the privilege of friendship and fellowship with the Supreme Creator of the universe who holds all things in the palms of His hands.

God comes to us personally when He says in the book of Jeremiah, "I satisfy the weary ones and refresh (fill) every one who languishes." That is His promise to us who hurt. David knew this. We can, too, as we take our thirsty souls to God:

> *O God, You are my God; I shall seek You earnestly;*
> *My soul thirsts for You, my flesh yearns for You,*
> *Thus I have seen You in the sanctuary,*
> *To see Your power and Your glory.*
> *Because Your lovingkindness is better than life,*
> *My lips will praise You.*
> *So I will bless You as long as I live;*
> *I will lift up my hands in Your name.*
> *My soul is satisfied as with marrow and fatness,*
> *And my mouth offers praises with joyful lips;*
> *When I remember You on my bed,*
> *I meditate on You in the night watches,*

For You have been my help,
And in the shadow of Your wings I sing for joy.
My soul clings to You;
Your right hand upholds me (Ps. 63:1-8).

In our loss, we gain a deep abiding relationship with our heavenly Father. While everything and every relationship in this life is fleeting and temporary, our relationship with God is permanent. We can run to Him with our longing heart, just as a child would run to his earthly father to soothe his hurts. Kay Arthur beautifully illustrates this in her personal story, "Running for Daddy!"

> When I was a little girl—just a skinny little beanpole with pigtails—I used to run to my daddy for comfort. I was a tomboy who consistently fell out of trees, got into fights, and crashed my bicycle. It seemed like I was forever bloodying those poor, banged-up knees of mine. That's when I would run—with pigtails flying and dirty tears streaming down my face—to my daddy.
>
> *"Daddy! Daddy! Daddy!"*
>
> And I'm so fortunate, because I had a daddy who held me. Ever since I was a little girl until the day he went to be with the Lord, I was always his little sweetheart. And I would fly into his open arms, and he would gather me up on his lap—dirt, blood, and all—and hold me there. And he would wipe my tears and push back my pigtails and say, "Now Honey, tell Daddy all about it."
>
> Many years later I was hurting again, so very deeply.
>
> But I couldn't run to my daddy.
>
> I was a single mom with two little kids, trying to work and go to school. And it was one of those days when everything seemed to catch up with me—all of the

hurt and loneliness and regret and pressure and weariness. I remember driving into the driveway of the little brick home where we were living. I got out of the car and began walking down the little gravel walkway toward the front door.

For some reason, time seemed to stand still for a moment.

To this day I can't tell you what triggered the thought, but suddenly—in my mind's eye—I saw something.

I saw a little girl, running,

I saw a little girl with tears streaming down her face and banged-up, bloody knees on those skinny little legs. I saw her in need of her daddy. Running for her daddy.

Then suddenly—strangely—I saw her running down a huge, shiny corridor. A vast corridor with gleaming marble walls and beautiful windows spilling heavenly light. And at the end of that marble hallway were massive doors of brilliant gold. Standing before those doors were bright, powerful guards with great spears.

And I knew that the little girl was me, and that I was running toward the very throne room of God, sovereign ruler of the universe. Yet I was the daughter of the King of Kings, so when the guards saw me coming, they swung open those doors and let me run in. There I was, weeping and running into the very presence of God. I heard the cherubim and the seraphim crying out, "Holy, holy, holy, Lord God Almighty! Heaven and earth are full of Thy glory!" Many bowed before the throne, and court was in session, but I just ran and ran and didn't stop...

I could just see myself running up the wide stairs to that glorious throne—two steps at a time—crying "Abba, Father! *Daddy!*"

And I could see Him stopping everything, opening His arms wide and just gathering me to His chest, saying, "There, there, My precious child. Let Me wipe away those tears. Tell your Father all about it."[4]

Yes, grief makes us hungry. It should. Healthy grieving arouses spiritual appetite. God wants that hunger to drive us to Himself, where we will find relief for our aching hearts in the warmth and love of our Father's arms.

Chapter Three

If Only, What If? But God!

*Grieve the past,
but don't get stuck.*

*B*rr... ing... Brr... ing. Martha picked up the telephone. Dad was on the other end. His voice was soft and serious.

"Sweetheart," Dad's voice cracked, "there's been a bad accident.... Your mother was coming home from her ladies' meeting and a truck hit her head-on. She... she was... killed instantly. I'm... I'm so sorry to have to tell you this, honey...." His voice trailed off like smoke from a chimney.

Martha's grip tightened on the phone. In her shock and utter disbelief, no words would come in response to her father's message. As both waited silently for the other to speak—to somehow right this awful wrong—tears of release flooded Martha's eyes and heavy, uncontrollable sobs took over. Dad joined in on the other end, as both father and daughter shared their grief.

"I'll pack and be there tonight," Martha finally managed to say. "I love you, Dad."

As Dad hung up, Martha stood there for a few seconds, as if in a trance, still clutching the receiver. The drone of the dial tone only seemed to reinforce the reality that Mom was gone. She was never coming back. *How could this be?* Martha pondered. A hundred questions invaded Martha's thoughts.

In the weeks that followed the funeral, Martha agonized over the *"if onlys." If only I hadn't said those harsh words to Mom the last time we spoke. If only we had spent more time together. If only I had been a better daughter.* Martha's *"if only"* thoughts became so obsessive, that she harbored needless guilt and anger leading to depression. Martha no longer functioned efficiently at work. Her marriage suffered. She fabricated excuses for staying home and avoided her friends. Martha's depression hindered her from acting in constructive ways. She rationalized to herself and others that she needed this time to be by herself. Martha felt so guilty as a result of her *"if onlys"* that she pushed everyone and everything she loved away.

Martha needed to grieve the past—the loss of her mother as well as the missing components of their relationship. She needed to forgive herself for not being the perfect daughter. Taking her guilt and anger to God in prayer would open up the door for His forgiveness and peace. Writing a letter to her deceased mother would help her articulate pent-up feelings that needed to get out in the open. Talking to at least one other trustworthy friend, perhaps her father, would bring further emotional healing.

Don't Dwell on the Future, But Hope in It

Equally as debilitating as living in the past is dwelling on the future. Have you ever met someone who is so consumed by the thought of a potential loss that it affects his entire life, as well as those around him? You probably have. He is the type of person most people avoid, because his pessimistic attitude clouds everyone else's day. A worry wart, we call him.

I shared a geometry class in high school with one of those compulsive individuals. She constantly anticipated a bad grade on the next test (even though she was a straight A student). Like a machine gun firing off rounds, she riddled the poor math teacher to death with every minute question she could think of, just to cover all the bases. Heavy groans, mingled with deep sighs, emanated from the back of the room. Even the teacher, normally thrilled to have students ask questions, uttered a few choice words under his breath and faced her with furrowed brow. This dear student feared losing her academic standing, and perhaps, in her mind, the respect of her parents, teacher, and classmates. Her anxiety over a grade left her constantly stuck in the future, bombarded by a barrage of *"what if"* questions. *What if I didn't study enough? What if I missed something in class that is on the test? What if I flunk this test?*

"What if" hinders a person from living life fully in the present. Abandonment to the will of God frees him to live the abundant life that Jesus said He came to give. To be free from *"what if"* anxiety, one must believe that God is in control and that He truly wants what is best for him. When a person has done all he reasonably knows to do to prevent a loss, he can pray the Serenity Prayer: "God, grant me the serenity to accept the things I cannot change, the courage to change the things I can, and the wisdom to know the difference."

Bathing our minds with Matthew 6:25-34 will ease *"what if"* anxiety and cause us to hope in God rather than dwell on possible loss scenarios:

> *For this reason I say to you, do not be worried about your life, as to what you will eat or what you will drink; nor for your body, as to what you will put on. Is not life more than food, and the body more than clothing? Look at the birds of*

the air, that they do not sow, nor reap nor gather into barns, and yet your heavenly Father feeds them. Are you not worth much more than they? And who of you by being worried can add a single hour to his life?

And why are you worried about clothing? Observe how the lilies of the field grow; they do not toil nor do they spin, Yet I say to you that not even Solomon in all his glory clothed himself like one of these. But if God so clothes the grass of the field, which is alive today and tomorrow is thrown into the furnace, will He not much more clothe you? You of little faith! Do not worry then, saying, "What will we eat?" or "What will we drink?" or "What will we wear for clothing?" For the Gentiles eagerly seek all these things; for your heavenly Father knows that you need all these things. But seek first His Kingdom and His righteousness, and all these things will be added to you. So do not worry about tomorrow; for tomorrow will care for itself. Each day has enough trouble of its own.

Another good passage for *"what if"* anxiety, written by the Apostle Paul while imprisoned, is Philippians 4:6-7: "Be anxious for nothing, but in everything by prayer and supplication with thanksgiving let your requests be made known to God. And the peace of God, which surpasses all comprehension, shall guard your hearts and your minds in Christ Jesus."

Embrace the Present

Relinquishing the *"if onlys"* and *"what ifs"* into God's safe keeping enables us to embrace the present. Repeatedly in Scripture, we can read about one Bible character after another who endured hard circumstances, faced wicked people, and suffered negative emotions, but God turned it all around for good.

I love the *"but God"* of Scripture. One of my favorite ones is found in Genesis 50:20 where Joseph responds to his brothers after they abused him and sold him into Egypt as a slave. Joseph says to them, "As for you, you meant evil against me, **but God** meant it for good in order to bring about this present result, to preserve many people alive (emphasis added)." God used Joseph's difficult circumstances to elevate him to a high ranking official in the Egyptian government. He was then in a position to use his God-given wisdom and skill to save lives, even the lives of his own family members, from the severe famine occurring during that time. Joseph had every reason to dwell in the past, but he did not. He embraced the present and God used him in the midst of his difficulty.

"*But God*" turns one's loss around and helps him see that God brings good out of the tragedy. He no longer needs to be stuck in the past or paralyzed by fear of the future. He knows that a wise and loving God is in control, a God who makes no mistakes, and works out His perfect plan for his life (Rom. 8:28). He then can deal in the present with the change that the loss has created. He realizes that change is necessary for growth.

Sometimes, God allows something to be taken from a person in order to get him out of a rut, to test his character, and reveal just what kind of progress is occurring in his spiritual life. He realizes that real change in his character only occurs through pain. The discipline of the loving, heavenly Father sometimes requires that we endure hardship in order to share in His holiness (Heb. 12:10).

What an awesome truth! We have the privilege of learning contentment by sharing in Christ's sufferings (Phil. 3:10). Then we can know His overcoming power in our lives in ways we never dreamed possible. I experienced a taste of this when I lost two babies through premature labor. Though I fought against the loss, God gently nudged me in His direction and lifted my heart upward to Him in a new and cherished way I have never forgotten.

At some point in the grieving process, we need to give ourselves permission to stop grieving and not feel guilty for doing so. We need to find safe people, places, and situations with whom to heal and encourage us. Finding opportunities to serve others can help ease our own pain. Sometimes "doing" things for others (like helping in a soup kitchen or taking a fruit basket to a sick friend) *before* we "feel" like it, is the ticket to our joy. There is joy and fulfillment in giving even while we still hurt. We can do these things now—in the present, even though the pain may still be intense. We can let go of the past, embrace the present, and hope in the future.

We can experience *good mourning*.

Part II

Building an Altar Out of Your Pain

It's doubtful that God can use any man greatly until he's hurt him deeply.

~A.W. Tozer~

Chapter Four

Memorial Stones to Wholeness

> There is no shortcut to wholeness:
> if you want to reach the Promised Land
> you must first go through the wilderness.
> ~Clifton Burke~

Your specific loss may not be mentioned in this book. The variety and range of loss is great. What we have endeavored to reveal through the few examples provided, is that whatever your loss, you share common feelings and adjustments with others. You have only to look around and realize that you are not alone. Hopefully, you will use the knowledge gained through your reading, to reach out to another hurting individual with a measure of understanding in your heart.

God's Trophy Case

In Hebrews 11, God provides His own list of hurting heroes who triumphed in their journey through the wilderness. We like to think of this grand display of characters as God's trophy case. God took each tarnished, smudged, and nicked individual, polished him and placed him on His shelf as an example for us to emulate. These trophies were not perfect. Some might look at the weaknesses of these men and women and scoff. They lied, cheated, doubted God, and committed immorality, but God, in His grace, used them in spite of their sin. God honored the faith that they had, and elevated them to status in the Hall of Faith for overcomers. These faithful servants looked past this world's loss to a heavenly world beyond.

How did these heroes of faith get to be heroes of faith? They lost something in order to gain something. And faith was the catalyst that ignited their passion and vision for God even in the midst of difficult circumstances.

We encourage you to spend some time studying the lives of these Hebrews 11 characters. Each is a story of pain and how God's strength triumphed over weakness. These faithful servants of the Old Testament were known for building altars to the Lord. Time and time again, they erected an altar as a result of their pain. They chose to praise and worship God even when they could not see the end result. They each walked through the painful wilderness to ultimately discover God's rich blessing. Final fulfillment of God's promise to them was not realized on this earth. Only when they stepped onto the portal of heaven did they fully understand God's dealings with them. Yet they chose to trust a God who promised to make good on His Word. The altar became a visual aid, symbolizing total abandonment of their broken bodies and souls to the Lord. The erected altar served as a memorial to God's faithfulness.

A Living Sacrifice

Thousands of years after the Old Testament saints walked the earth, the Apostle Paul urged the Church to build an altar. He spoke of a living sacrifice offered through an act of the will, not upon a physical altar but a spiritual one. As a Christian, I say, "I do," to the Lordship of Christ. I figuratively climb up on the altar, dying to self, in order that I might truly live for Christ. Paul urges in Romans 12:1-2,

> ...to present your bodies a living and holy sacrifice, acceptable to God, which is your spiritual service of worship. And do not be conformed to this world, but be transformed by the renewing of your mind, so that you may prove what the will of God is, that which is good and acceptable and perfect.

I take the hard, cold, ugly rocks, representing each loss, and I begin laying them, one by one, on top of each other as a memorial of how God, in my brokenness, delivered me as I presented each hurt to Him. Paul knew what it meant to be broken and spilled out for the Lord. In Galatians 6:17, he said that he bore the brandmarks of Jesus on his body. Because of his service for the Lord, he carried literal scars from beatings and imprisonment. From his cell, he wrote to the Philippian Church about contentment, and about the loss of all things in order to gain Christ.

Paul also remembered that even the resurrected Lord, in His glorious body, still bore the scars of the nails in His hands and side. Throughout all eternity, His scars would serve as a visual aid, reminding us of God's victorious deliverance over sin and the grave. Jesus did not hide His scars; neither did Paul, and neither should we, by the way. Allow the scars to be reminders of God's working in your life—how He delivered you from sadness, anger, or bitterness. God *can* enter through our brokenness, when we offer ourselves as a living sacrifice on an altar of total abandonment to His purposes.

Paul understood, as did our Hebrews 11 crew, that he belonged to another world. Knowing heaven was his real home, kept him strong through the pain and disappointment of this life.

Building an altar out of your pain may be difficult. Hundreds of cold, ugly rocks line your pathway blocking your view of God.

Only when you begin picking them up, one by one, and presenting them to God can you finally see Him.

I counseled one man who had been abused as a child. Because he had not dealt with the abuse, his hurts had accumulated over time, finally leading him to my office. His rocks included loss of innocence as a child, loss of respect, loss of identity, and later a loss of physical function. He was angry at his abuser and felt controlled by her. Based on Romans 12:1-2, I led him to build an altar with all the rocks of his life.

When building an altar, you have to accept that God is in control and protects you from too much pain, even the pain that comes from others and is sometimes the result of sin. You might ask, "Why didn't God keep this awful thing from happening?" I don't know, but if God allowed it to happen, He can, in His sovereignty, bring good from it (see Rom. 8:28). Even though you cannot always give thanks for the hurts themselves, you can always give thanks for the God who loves you and cares about every minute detail of your life.

In her book, *God of All Comfort,* Hannah Whitall Smith offers the following perspective:

> God may not have ordered them (the losses), but He is in them somewhere, and He is in them to compel, even the most grievous, to work together for our good. The "second causes" of the wrong may be full of malice and wickedness, but faith never sees second causes. It sees only the hand of God behind the second causes. They are all under His control, and not one of them can touch us except with His knowledge and permission. The thing itself that happens cannot perhaps be said to be the will of God, but by the time its effects reach us they have become God's will for us, and must be accepted as from His hands.[1]

Remember Joseph in the book of Genesis. Rejected by his jealous brothers, sold into Egypt as a slave, falsely accused by Potiphar's wife, and thrown into prison unjustly, he had his share of cold, ugly rocks. But Joseph knew God had a purpose in allowing each loss. When Joseph's brothers came to Egypt seeking food during the severe famine, and Joseph finally revealed who he was, the brothers feared for their lives. Because God had His hand on Joseph, He had elevated him to a high position in the Egyptian government. His brothers had reason to fear. They thought for sure Joseph would use his power to get even. Who in his right mind wouldn't? But Joseph, enabled by God's hand, said to them, "You meant evil against me, but God meant it for good" (Gen. 50:20).

Joseph had taken all the evil rocks and built an altar. He then climbed up on the altar, demonstrating total trust in God's purposes. He was willing to embrace his current identity. He exhibited a contentment that allowed him to make his life count in the midst of the pain.

Visualize yourself picking up each loss of your life and stacking each one, forming an altar to God. See yourself climbing the altar and lying down, face pointed heavenward. When you are lying on the altar, your face is looking up to God. You acknowledge that He is in control, that He cares and loves you, that He is trustworthy. Building an altar gives purpose to your pain. Visualizing your presentation to God brings a sense of freedom. You are no longer denying the loss or pretending the pain is not real. You tell the truth about each hurt and give it to God. God enables you to do this by His mercy. You present all that you are—a complete package.

Since Christ fully presented Himself as a sacrifice for your wholeness, peace, and well-being, presenting yourself is the very least you can do in response to Christ's love for you. In fact, it is the only thing you can do and it is all God requires that you do.

For then you are in a position of blessing. God takes your offering and makes something beautiful out of it.

As you present yourself, lean hard on God. Refuse to listen to the world's message or Satan's lies. Listen to God's Word and meditate on His promises. Renew your mind daily by quoting Scripture. Then you will learn how God can use your losses for His glory.

I won't forget my losses. Neither will you. But God can turn the memory into healing as we offer the broken pieces of our lives to God. Only then can we experience true wholeness.

Part III

Special Kinds of Losses

Chapter Five

Living With an Illness

> The greatest sermons I have ever heard
> were not preached from pulpits
> but from sickbeds.
> ~M.R. DeHaan~

The anxious crowd gathers around as Jesus steps out of the boat and onto the Galilean seashore. Like an eager throng welcoming a war hero home, this exuberant multitude receives their hometown boy back to Capernaum. They press in harder, questioning Jesus about His latest miracle. Suddenly, a man named Jairus emerges from the crowd and falls at Jesus' feet. He pleads with Jesus to come to his home where his only daughter lay dying. Without a second thought, Jesus walks with the man.

The crazed crowd, hungry to see Jesus perform another miracle, push and shove one another to stay on top of Him. They flock around their hero, hemming Him in, as they shuffle in one big bunch to the emergency scene.

Unexpectedly, Jesus stops short, turns, and says, "Who touched Me?" His abrupt question startles the group, who amusingly enough, deny any possible physical contact. Even Peter retorts, "Master, the multitudes are crowding and pressing upon You." In other words, *Get real, You've got to be kidding. This many people crammed together and You ask who touched Me! Unbelievable!*

Jesus, however, insists that someone did touch Him, for He was aware that power had gone out of Him. His searching eyes scan the crowd. That penetrating gaze is more than the offending party can tolerate. A woman, trembling with fear and guilt, desperately makes her way through the onlookers and falls down before Jesus. Before He has a chance to say anything, the woman nervously rattles off her woeful tale about the physical misery she has endured for the last twelve years. A news hungry reporter inches his way through the crowd, leaning in to listen as he advances. He grabs his pen and pad and scribbles down distorted notes for the next issue of his tabloid. *Ah, this would make a juicy story,* he drools to himself. Dollar signs dance before his eyes, adding to his thirst for the woman's revealing story.

The woman spills the whole truth of how she had endured a chronic uterine hemorrhage, how she had sought out every possible remedy known to the medical profession, and how she had spent her entire life's savings doing so. She not only was not cured, but had actually grown worse as a result of the treatments. Because of the hygienic requirements of the Mosaic Law, she had been ostracized by her husband, family, and community. She was literally an outcast. She was forbidden to touch anyone, and no one was permitted to touch her.

Whispers rumble through the crowd as the woman bares her soul. She stands emotionally naked before the accusing group. Men sneer at her. Women turn their backs in disgust. Following their parents' example, children mock and jeer. In this Eastern culture, her particular ailment was considered a result of an immoral lifestyle. She was not even allowed to worship in the synagogue. She was stripped of her dignity and forced into isolation. She had nowhere else to turn and no one who would receive her.

Then Jesus steps onto the canvas of her painful life and offers in one swift brush stroke the prospect of a new portrait. She had heard about the many healings. Just maybe Jesus could heal her. Could it be possible? She held out hope just one more time. That hope had led her to join the crowd that day.

Hope strengthened her weakness, propelling her through the tight throng. Coming up behind Jesus, she reached out in a last ditch effort and seized the tassel swinging from His robe as He inched through the crowd. Ironically, this very tassel, one of four, with a blue cord running through, was sewn on the corner of the outer cloak to remind the children of Israel to keep God's commandments—to be holy, even as He is holy. In the face of that reality, this poor, destitute woman literally clutched the symbol representing everything pure and godly.

As the woman continues her story, the horrified crowd stops breathing. In their eyes, she had committed an abomination. Surely, Jesus would reprimand her and send her away. Not so.

Instead, Jesus looks into her pleading eyes and speaks reassuring words, "Daughter, your faith has made you well; go in peace" (Luke 8:48*).* Jesus offers the hurting woman a deep abiding assurance and confidence that her healing is permanent. He frees her from guilt over her secret way of securing her cure without His consent, something that may have concerned her. Furthermore, Jesus assures her that she is clean and will remain so. She need not worry about making someone else unclean. He calls her *daughter*, indicating not only that physical healing took place, but also spiritual healing. Jesus emphasizes that it is her faith that made her well, not any superstitious idea that a mere touch of a tassel could generate healing.

By now, the astonished crowd stands with gaping mouths and tied tongues. They utter no words. The reporter's pen slips from his hand and onto the sandy ground. In the stillness, I hear Jesus utter to the woman, "Where are your accusers?" and because there are none, He says, "Go in peace."

Jesus knew the difference between the pressing crowd and the touch of a needy person expressing faith. Even though He is on an urgent call to heal a dying child, He takes time to stop along the way and help another hurting soul. This ailing woman had a personal encounter with the Great Physician. Jesus lingers long enough to have a one-on-one encounter with this no-name woman. Her faith, prompted by desperation and, perhaps, mingled with superstition, pressed her to seek Jesus. In spite of her fear, public confession followed genuine inner faith. She embarked on a whole new way of life, spiritually, as well as physically, for she had met the One who understood her pain and delivered her from it.

Jesus Understands

Like the woman, it is easy during an illness to become frustrated and discouraged over the duration of the ailment. Day after agonizing day drags by without relief. From the sick-bed, one looks out his bedroom window and sees the sun rise, the sun set, and still no change. Often the doctors are in a quandary as to how to help, experimenting with one drug, surgery, or therapy after another as financial resources plummet to an all-time low. The cost of a certain treatment exceeds the customary allotted fee established by the insurance company, and the desperate patient ends up owing a huge amount of out-of-pocket expense.

The sick one feels isolated by family as he hears them go about their daily routine without him. He feels guilty because he cannot carry his share of the load. Social outings with friends are now restricted or non-existent, because his pain or disability is too debilitating. In his loneliness, he is tempted to ask "Why me?"

Just like the ailing woman in Scripture, his faith is put to the test at his weakest point. He now has a choice. Will he seek Jesus at the first sign of pain? Or will he turn his back on God, blaming and accusing Him for the illness? Blaming God or anyone else will drive him to further discomfort, as emotional pain unites with his physical pain, sending him spiraling down the dark tunnel of despair. Seeking Jesus at the first sign of pain, even before he has exhausted all his human wisdom and financial resources, is always the best choice. Jesus stands ready to touch any person, at any time, in any place with the gift of His love, peace, and stability.

For whatever reason, Jesus does not always heal every illness. God usually allows the physical laws of the universe to run their course. If someone has a flu virus, God is not going to miraculously take the ailment away. The disease will need to run its course, not because the person sinned, but because he came into contact with the flu virus. Some conditions will find ultimate healing in heaven. Though we may not understand, God's timing is always right and good, and perfectly suited to our individual needs.

Jairus must have at least inwardly questioned the Master's timing on the way to heal his little girl—the cherished apple of his eye. In the urgency of the moment, Jairus must have wondered how Jesus could possibly stop and help an undeserving, outcast woman who had lived through her illness, an illness that apparently was not life threatening. *After all*, he must have speculated, *she's already dealt with this for twelve years; she will survive a little while longer. My daughter is close to death. I need Jesus more than she does.* Notice how pain can often make one selfish, if he succumbs to its power.

Jesus performed abundant physical healings during His earthly ministry in order to authenticate His message—that He truly was the Messiah, the Son of God. Through the power of His Spirit, He passed the healing touch on to His disciples after He ascended back to heaven—all for the purpose of authenticating His message. He wanted hurting people to know in a tangible way that He was indeed the Son of the Living God. This was significant to that particular age, since the people only had the first five books of the Law.

In our present age, we have the completed revelation of God, the Bible in sixty-six books, to offer us all the verification we need that, yes, Jesus is indeed the Son of the Living God. He no longer walks among us, publicly curing ills at the touch of His hand, but we have the witness of His followers down through the ages, under divine inspiration, to assure us that He is who He claims to be. Though at times, we may long for His physical presence and healing touch, He has chosen to work through His written Word in this dispensation. Sometimes, He will physically cure an illness in answer to prayer or through medical or alternative health intervention. Sometimes, He does not. The *"whys"* flood in around us during those times and clamor for answers.

When a person allows his pain to be his teacher, he learns sooner or later, that the *"why,"* which he may never discover, is not nearly as important as the *"Who."* Leaning hard on God, learning more of Him—*"Who"* He is and what He offers—is of extreme importance during times of pain. Delving into Scripture, he discovers that God always works for His glory, for a person's spiritual growth, to silence Satan, as in the case of Job, for a testimony to unbelievers, and to encourage believers in their faith walk.

I remember a minor surgery I underwent four years ago. I know now that whenever a doctor says, "minor," you can take it to the bank that he really means, "major." Anytime one submits to anesthetic, it's major. My recuperation time, which was supposed to last only a few days, extended into two-and-a-half weeks. I literally rolled on the bed in pain. All I could do was look up. Nothing helped. I could hear Chuck and the girls playing ball out in our back yard. I wondered how they could have so much fun when I was in agony inside. I felt left out. I would have been angry, but I was in too much pain to care.

Even when I couldn't read the Bible or pray for very long because of the intense pain, God was faithful to me. When I least expected it, Jesus came to me and offered me a fresh glimpse of Himself. Oh, not in a physical sense. I did not literally see Him in my room. But I did sense His presence, which I don't think could have been more real if He had stepped out of heaven and into the room with me. I saw Him suffering on the cross with the nails piercing His hands and feet, struggling to lift Himself to gasp one more life-giving breath. I heard Him cry out in agony, "My God, my God, why have You forsaken Me?" In that revealing moment, I knew my Jesus understood my pain, more than the doctors, more than my caring family, more than my sweet brothers and sisters in Christ. He had experienced the depths of pain, by His own choice—for me. He had been where I was now and so much deeper. He understood.

I recovered from my brief illness with a greater appreciation for those who are chronic sufferers. I gained a deeper love for the caring ministry of the Body of Christ and my own dear family. Most of all, I fell in love with my Lord all over again, but with more intensity, and fervency, and conviction that He is with me through all of life's crises.

Someday, when I get to heaven, I want to look up that woman with no name. I'm sure I'll see a bright twinkle in her eye as she recounts the day she had faith enough to reach out to Jesus and receive an everlasting cure. In a moment of reverent silence, we'll grab each other and hug, as only two can who share a common Love.

Dealing With the Pain, Loneliness, and Depression

Perhaps you are reading this chapter as one who has suffered a chronic illness for years. Be encouraged—others have been where you are, and most importantly, Jesus understands your heartache better than anyone else. You have gleaned rich truths from the Lord during your confinement. You have encouraged others through your life of quiet submission to God's plan. But you, too, need some uplift today. Below are some tips gleaned from others who have endured long illness or handled lifelong handicaps. You could probably add a few helpful insights of your own.

1. Learn to accept the reality of your illness or handicap. If it is a permanent condition, then you will have to grieve the primary physical loss as well as multiple secondary losses. If the illness is terminal, as with cancer, you must learn to accept death as a natural part of life. Seek help making practical arrangements for your will and funeral. You are in the position to plan a service that would be exactly what you want as a testimony of God's working in your life.

2. Talk to God about your illness. Let Him know exactly how you feel, no matter how ugly. Get the truth out on the table. Then God can help you work through your varied emotions.

Study His Word. If you are physically unable to read, then listen to Scripture tapes and Christian radio. Have a friend over to read the Word to you and pray. God will shed light on His plan for your illness and how you can bring glory to His name in the midst of it. He will reveal to you that, as you are an example to others in your endurance, you are heaping up for yourself heavenly glory beyond comprehension (2 Cor. 4:17). Just as Paul learned contentment through the things he suffered, so can you as you present your weakness to God. He will prove His grace sufficient for you, for His power is perfected in weakness in such a way that you will no longer glory in yourself, but in the Christ who indwells you (2 Cor. 12:9-10).

3. Become a fervent prayer warrior for others. It may be the greatest work you ever do. While many in good health don't feel they have the time to invest in prayer, God has opened an exciting door of ministry for you, a ministry that is sorely needed in a day when everyone seems to be in a hurry. Those who suffer are often the best and most effective pray-ers, fueling God's work from their beds. God's Church would be powerless without the faithful prayers of these shut-ins.

4. Keep a positive attitude. Over the years, we have been greatly inspired by our cerebral palsy friend, Deb, who encourages others to "keep on keeping on" in the face of limitation. She advises others to view their disability as a gift from God. She has been able to minister to people that she probably would never have had the opportunity to reach, if it had not been for her disability. She also encourages others to simply take one day at a time, and to dwell on the good things God has given.

Good mental health can promote physical healing. Even though you may have people trying to lift your spirits, learn to cheer yourself on. Be your own best support system. Give yourself a hug. Say encouraging statements to yourself right out loud. Don't succumb to feelings of inferiority as you view those around you functioning normally. Insist to yourself and verbalize to others that God is using you today. Flush out pent-up feelings of resentment or bitterness. Confess them to God and be rid of them. Many degenerative diseases can be traced to harboring negative feelings.

5. Do something for someone else today. Don't view your worth based on physical productiveness, but rather on matters of the heart. In other words, give someone else an encouraging word today, a smile, a pat on the shoulder. Sometimes, a listening ear is the greatest gift you could offer another person in a day and age when no one has time to sit down and really focus in on another person.

If you can use your hands, write a letter or brief note to another shut-in or hurting person. Include some Scriptures or ways God has helped you. What a treat to receive a personal handwritten note from a caring person that you know is in the midst of pain himself! It creates a genuine spiritual bond.

6. Join a support group for those suffering from a common illness or handicap. Connecting with others regularly, who are going through a similar crisis can be a boost for you. As trust builds, you can learn to share your feelings openly, as well as encourage others. You may leave the meeting feeling that your life is not quite as bad as you thought.

7. Determine what you can do and set goals for yourself. Jean Driscoll, two-time Olympic silver medalist, born with spina bifida, and confined to a wheelchair says:

> "Anytime I'm having a bad workout or I don't feel like doing something, I remember what Jesus said in John 17:4. He was praying to God the Father, and He said: 'I have brought you glory on earth by completing the work you gave me to do (NIV).' That verse reminds me that I'm doing the work God has called me to do. I just have to do that, and He takes care of the details!"[1]

Resist the temptation to make others feel sorry for you. Don't make them be responsible for you every minute of every day. You will feel more in control, and everyone involved will be the freer for it.

Don't compare yourself with other people. Accept your limitations, but also recognize the gifts God has given you, and the unique position in which He has placed you to express those gifts.

Everyone is facing some kind of problem situation in his life. Yours just happens to be a chronic illness. That makes you no better or no worse off than anyone else. In other words, don't harbor a distorted image of yourself. Allow God to make all things clear.

He may use other people to help you. Be open to what they share and, before God, consider the validity of their advice. Accept your difficulty as a challenge for inner growth and renewal, an opportunity you may not have received were you in an upright position walking on two legs.

Set goals for yourself, but don't be discouraged if you fail. Simply rework your goal and try again. But never stop trying. There can be no failure as long as you begin afresh.

8. If you are married, allow the illness to strengthen your marriage, rather than tear it down. Obviously, there are unique stressors to an ongoing illness. Tempers flare, nerves are on edge, and exhaustion sets in for the sick one as well as the caregiver. Care over choice of words, that should be taken in every relationship, is now even more important with the added stress of an illness.

Don't be afraid to ask for outside help when needed, either from your church or community agencies. No man is an island. Share the load. Talk with each other candidly, but thoughtfully, about your feelings concerning the illness, your individual roles within the household, and your future.

Seek creative ways to reach out together beyond your front door. As people visit, initiate a prayer circle, and pray for others' needs as well as your own.

Read together. Listen to good music together. Work a puzzle. Watch a funny movie. Bring candles into the sickroom and cuddle for awhile. In short, find things you can do together **now** to enhance your relationship. They may not be the things you used to do, but with some creative brainstorming, you will find new endeavors.

One mate's confinement can actually lend itself to a deeper, more meaningful relationship, if the other mate will seek the opportunity to be with the ailing partner at points during the day or evening.

9. Take charge of your health. Do your research. Seek out possible alternatives to traditional medicines, especially if you are finding no help from them. There are many good alternative health programs in existence, but the one we have discovered most beneficial to long term healing is the one endorsed by Dr. George Malkmus, founder of Hallelujah Acres, and author of several books, including *God's Way to Ultimate Health*. I strongly recommend his health plan. It may just be the secret to your healing.

10. Invest in laughter every day. It may be the best gift you give yourself and those around you. Maybe you have seen the movie, *Patch Adams*. Based on the true story of a medical student who uses humor to promote healing, the movie portrays his struggle against the traditional idea of the stoic, elevated tradition of white coats and impersonal methods. In danger of being kicked out of medical school, he confronts the authorities with a moving speech in defense of his methodology, resulting in respect from his mentors and his ultimate graduation. He goes on to create a successful practice, employing heavy doses of therapeutic laughter and a personal touch unparalleled by any in his field. Dr. Adams had tapped into a secret well-worth discovering—the healing power of laughter.

Because laughter releases endorphins in the brain which bathe the body with natural pain relief, many sufferers have found that a few minutes of hearty laughter a day can actually free them from time spent in pain. So, find a good, side-splitting movie to watch tonight, and hunker down for some much needed pain relief. Or better yet, read a good clean joke book and try some out on your spouse tonight. Never is a good sense of humor more needed than when one suffers from a chronic ailment.

11. If you are physically able, get some exercise every day. Even if all you can do is wiggle your toes, do finger bends, or raise your eyebrows repeatedly—DO IT! If nothing else, the effort will make you laugh! Remember the friendly endorphins. They are also released during exercise, so get involved.

12. Breathe. This may seem like a paradox. *What do you mean, breathe?* you might be thinking. *I may be barely alive, but I know I am breathing!* Yes, you are breathing, but do you know how many of us go about our daily activities breathing in a shallow, half-hearted manner? No wonder we feel sluggish most of the time. Inadequate oxygen is getting to our organs. We need to practice deep breathing every day, preferably twice a day to enhance our physical health.

Stop right now and practice. Breathe in slowly through your nose to the count of four. Hold it for seven seconds. Then, slowly exhale through your mouth to the count of eight, making a whooshing sound as you expel the air. At the beginning, do this four times two times a day. Then, increase this exercise to eight times two times a day. Feel the tension and stress leave your body as the oxygen courses through your veins, flooding every inch of your being with life-giving rejuvenating power.

13. Know when to seek professional help. If you find you are not able to eat, sleep, or enjoy life to any degree, then it is time for professional help.

❦

There was once a clock pendulum waiting to be fixed. It began to calculate how long it would be expected to tick day and night, so many times a minute, sixty times every hour, twenty-four hours every day, and three hundred and sixty-five times every year. It was awful! Enough to stagger the mind. Millions of ticks!

"I can never do it," said the poor pendulum. But the clockmaster encouraged it.

"Do just one tick at a time," he said. "That is all that will be required of you."

So the pendulum went to work, one tick at a time, and it is ticking yet.

(Anon)

Perhaps that is all you can do today, dear hurting one—simply one tick at a time. May God bless you as you reach out to Jesus in your illness or handicap. May He bless your life in ways you never dreamed possible. May He remove the scales from your eyes that hinder you from seeing His face clearly. May you be a better, stronger person for what you have endured. May you feel the Savior's warm, loving embrace envelop you in a special way right this moment. Though you remain faceless to us, may you feel our support in prayer and thought. If you would like, write to us. We will share in mutual encouragement, for we are all a needy people.

Chapter Six

Moving to a New City

*Our Lord did not ask us to give up the things of earth,
but to exchange them for better things.*
~Fulton J. Sheen~

      *S*arai nestles in closer to Abram as they gaze into the night fire. The cool air sends chills down their spines as they pull the blanket tighter around them. Tomorrow they will be leaving Ur and moving to Canaan. The God of glory had appeared to Abram and said, "Depart from your country and your relatives, and come into the land that I will show you."

Abram and Sarai reflect on what they will be leaving behind. Together, with Abram's father, Terah, and his brothers, they had grown wealthy and prosperous in a land of idolatry. They had lifelong friends in Ur. They had made a home for themselves. Emotions run rampant. A hundred questions flood their minds as they consider the approaching morn.

Yet God had called them to be a separated people unto Himself and they must go.

Gleanings from Genesis 12-20

> *Now the Lord said to Abram, "Go forth from your country, and from your relatives and from your father's house, To the land which I will show you; And I will make you a great nation, and I will bless you, and make your name great; And so you shall be a blessing; And I will bless those who bless you, and the one who curses you I will curse. And in you all the families of the earth will be blessed"* (Gen. 12:1-3).

Notice in these verses that God replaces every loss associated with Abram's move with a gain.

- Abram leaves a familiar country to become a great nation.
- Abram leaves his family to be blessed with a posterity beyond comprehension.
- Abram leaves his home to establish a new home where his name will be great and ultimately all the families of the earth will be blessed.

Five times in this passage, God says that He *will* bless Abram. God *will* do what is beyond Abram's control. God *will* provide the new land, family, and nation. *God will do it!* Abram's job is simply to respond in faith. Abram is put to the test. Does he love God more than home and family?

In spite of God's assurance, Abram shows partial obedience to God's call. Genesis 12:1 indicates that God called Abram to leave *all* his family members behind, except for his wife, Sarai. God could not bless Abram until he had separated from the wicked, idolatrous lifestyle of his father's house. Yet, Abram leaves Ur with his father, Terah, and nephew, Lot. This act of divided allegiance only serves to complicate the move for Abram.

Abram and his family make it as far as Haran, a few miles from Ur, and settle there until the death of his father. At this point,

Abram sets out for Canaan with Sarai, Lot, and all the possessions and servants he had accumulated in Haran. Abram still responds in partial obedience, but he is headed in the right direction. As we observe the lives of Abram and Lot as they journey from their homeland, we discover some striking differences in the character of both men.

Abram chooses a spiritual lifestyle. Lot chooses a carnal, worldly lifestyle. The Lord knows He can entrust Abram with His divine promise. Abram has a personal relationship with the Lord. He not only knows God, he has a personal encounter with God on a regular basis. Upon entering the land of Canaan, Abram's first act is building an altar to worship his God (Gen. 12:7). No such record is given of Lot, who, though righteous, has no spiritual discernment. The only indication we are given from Scripture that Lot has any kind of relationship with God, is that he is rescued from Sodom, for God promised to deliver the righteous from destruction (Gen. 18-19).

Abram acts out of gratefulness. Lot acts out of greed. God promises the entire land of Canaan to Abram and his descendants. Abram has every right to hoard the land for himself. Abram could have said to Lot, "Hey, this land is mine. You'll take what I give you. No more. No less." But no, Abram turns right around and offers Lot first dibs on land, allowing him to settle his family, servants, and herds wherever he chooses (Gen. 13:9-11). Gratefulness to God breeds generosity. Sadly, Lot's greedy heart takes full advantage of Abram's generosity.

Abram is concerned about personal integrity. Lot is concerned about personal prosperity. While Abram makes some poor judgment calls during this period in his life (Gen. 12:10-20), his overriding lifestyle reflects a depth of character committed to doing God's will. His sin against Sarai, while in Egypt, results in repentance. He immediately leaves Egypt and returns to Bethel, "to the place of the altar... and there Abram called on the name of the Lord" (Gen. 13:4). Never once do we find Lot on his face before God in repentance or worship. Never once do we read of Lot checking into the moral disposition of Sodom before he moves his family there. He is only concerned about the material benefits the physical land offers, such as plenty of water and lush, green grass for his flocks.

Abram intercedes on Lot's behalf more than once, through diplomacy (Gen. 13), through physical force (Gen. 14), and, on another occasion, through direct supplication on Lot's behalf for deliverance from Sodom (Gen. 18). Lot never learns to seek God's direction, nor listen for His voice. Lot focuses on what he can get out of life. Abram focuses on God, and thus develops a giving spirit.

Abram gains materially and morally. Lot loses materially and morally. It is only when Abram separates himself from Lot that God is able to bless him fully (Gen. 13:14-18). Abram's response to God's blessing is to once again build an altar. Abram proves himself a man of faith. Lot is merely a man of sight. He hungers for what he sees, and, ultimately, ends up losing everything that he has acquired and considers so essential to his happiness.

According to Peter's account in 2 Peter 2:7-8, Lot soon discovers that his supposed gain in Sodom is actually a terrible loss. He is oppressed day after day by homosexuals, filthy talk, lawlessness, and fleshly desires of all kinds. But Lot is so attached to the world that, even when the angels come to deliver him and his family from Sodom's destruction, he hesitates. The angels literally seize him by the hand and pull him out of the wicked city (Gen. 19:15-16). God's compassion is indeed great! Abram's love and patience for his wayward nephew is moving as he intercedes to God on his behalf.

Lot loses his sons-in-law, his wife, his home, his possessions, and shortly thereafter, the moral integrity of his two daughters who commit incest to preserve the family. His girls had been so influenced by the lack of morality in Sodom, that they were able to commit such a godless act without the blink of an eyelash (Gen. 19:34-36). High price to pay for material greed.

I can't help but wonder what poor, disillusioned Lot was thinking about, all alone in his cave, far from Sodom with no wife to comfort him, and all his worldly treasures gone in a puff of smoke and ash. The Scriptures are silent as to Lot's future. There is no record of his ever turning to God in his desperation, or building an altar to worship the Lord. He is left in a dark, dank, musty cave, a broken disheveled man, who drifts off into obscurity, never to be heard of again.

What a different portrait we have of Abram's future! The recipient of God's blessing, he goes on to become the father of a great nation. Along the way, he is found interceding again on the behalf of those in need (Gen. 20:17).

Though separated from us by thousands of years, the biblical account of Abram and Lot provides timely instruction for anyone considering a move.

Questions to Ponder

Several questions rise to the surface based on our study of Abram and Lot. When considering a move to a new city, ask yourself the following:

1. Have I consulted God in my decision-making?

Matthew 6:33 admonishes us to seek God's Kingdom first, and then He will provide all that we need here on earth. When we get our priorities out of order and seek temporal prosperity first, we may, in the end, lose our worldly possessions. As believers in the Lord Jesus Christ, we recognize His Lordship over our lives. We belong to Him. We look for a city whose builder is God, for our real home is in heaven (Heb. 11:10). Where He leads down here, is inconsequential, for we realize that it is merely a temporary home.

Colossians 3:1-2 urges us to set our affections on things above. If we do this, we lose a worldly focus and gain a heavenly vision. When we delight ourselves in the Lord, exemplified by our desire to spend time with Him in His Word and prayer, then He will give us the desires of our hearts (Ps. 37:4). The more intimacy we have with our Lord, the more His desires become our desires. We want the same things. It becomes easy for God to direct us when we are on the same wave length, united in thought and purpose.

Once God has provided specific direction, we need to obey Him fully, entrusting every detail of the move to His care. Rarely do we understand ahead of time, how everything about the move is going to play out. Abram did not. We won't either. Walking by faith, rather than by sight, is essential to our spiritual and emotional well-being.

2. How will I provide for the moral development of my children?

Lot had obviously been given a choice in his move. He chose Sodom, not God. He did not even check into the spiritual atmosphere of the city, before moving his wife and daughters there. Lot sinks deeper, when he has the unspiritual gall to offer his two daughters to the wicked men of the city in order to save his own hide. Lot's heart is so far from God by the time the angels arrive to deliver him, that they literally have to seize him by the hand to remove him from Sodom.

The progression of Lot's spiritual demise is a sad one, and, perhaps, totally unnecessary, had he done his homework before the move. He acted on impulse, without a thought about the influence such a place would have on his growing family.

3. Have I considered the advice of those closest to me?

Lot did not. Don't make the same mistake.

When we were praying about a move to Alabama a few years ago, we included our three girls in the decision-making process. We had several meetings around our dining room table, praying and discussing the potential move and thrashing out the pros and cons. Together, we came up with a sheet of written positives and negatives about the move. Each item was assigned a number on a scale of one to ten, one being least important and ten being most important. Each person tallied his sheet privately and, then, we met together again as a family. The resulting score revealed that we were not ready to make a move at that time. The position offered might be in our family's future, but the timing was not right just then.

4. Can I serve God more effectively if I move?

God called Abram out of pagan Ur so that He could bless him personally as well as nationally. The blessing extended to all aspects of his life. Obedience to God's purpose yields His blessing, even when we do not understand all His directives. We merely act on what we do know, put one foot in front of the other, and He directs our way, one step at a time. It is a blessing, in and of itself, to rely on Him so totally, for indeed as Deuteronomy 30:19-20 tells us—He is our very survival, our life! And His Word promises us that He makes no mistakes. Just as with Abram, He can be our trusted friend. We can confide in Him about every detail and every feeling surrounding the move. God's plan for Abram could not be fulfilled until he made the first step. We must be willing to do the same.

5. What is my purpose in moving?

Ask God to reveal to you any hidden motives in the move that you may not be aware of. Is more money or a higher level job your motive? Or do you desire a quiet spot in the country without the bother of neighbors? Neither of these motives is necessarily wrong. The secret is testing each motive in the light of God's Word, and bathing each desire in prayer. Listening for the inner voice of the Spirit in prayer is as important as talking to God in prayer.

Ask God to specifically reveal to you anything that might hinder His perfect will from being accomplished. Then watch to see how God does that! He may bring another believer into your life who raises some red flags concerning the move. Or He may confirm the move through two or three other believers, who you know are walking close to the Lord. Take their advice seriously and weigh it out before the Lord. You have asked for God's direction. He is faithful to provide it. Once you have determined that a move is God's will for you at this time, be prepared to grieve the loss of your current home.

Practical Advice

A common feeling courses through the veins of those we have talked with who have moved. They each share a mixture of excitement and apprehension. Excitement at the thought of a new start in a totally new place. Apprehension at leaving friends, family, stores, doctors, familiar places, and a church to which they are accustomed.

Feelings of loneliness, separation, and insecurity can shroud the anticipated move and crop up at unexpected times. It is important to recognize a move, however major or minor, as a form of loss which must be grieved fully. Sometimes, that is difficult in the flurry of activity accompanying relocation. Often, our grief is not fully felt until the move is complete and our life is re-established in a new place. This can require months of searching out new stores, churches, doctors, dentists, and a host of other resources.

I remember when we made our last move. Not being one for finding my way easily, I drove around Roanoke for an hour, trying to locate a car repair shop for a shattered Pontiac window. My three young daughters gladly aided me, by occasionally tossing out a helpful statement from the backseat, like, "Didn't we pass that Burger King just a little bit ago?" Seething under my breath, I muttered to myself, *Yes, we did—only five times now!*

"Movers" share some helpful tips on easing the transition, especially when tempers are short and anxiety runs high.

Talk out your feelings. Once a fairly comfortable routine is underway in the new household, overwhelming feelings of loss can bear down upon us. Journaling our feelings, talking them out with the family and God, and forming new attachments are helpful ways to deal with "moving" grief.

Take steps to adjust emotionally. Recognize that, as with any grief, it will take time to adjust emotionally to the move. Be patient with yourself. Don't wait for people to come to you. Take steps to reach out to your new neighbors. Visit several churches, but don't wait too long to re-establish yourself in a local body of believers. You need them and they need you. Don't cheat yourself out of a major source of God's blessing for your life. Getting involved quickly in the lives of other people will ease any depressing feelings you may have surrounding the move.

Be especially sensitive to the feelings of young children. Though you may have only been in a certain location for a few years, to your child, it is a lifetime. Help ease his anxiety by hosting a farewell party for his friends. Take pictures and help him make a scrapbook of his old home and friends. When it comes time to move, let him choose a box to pack his personal belongings in. He may even enjoy decorating it. Once the move is made, help ease his transition by doing familiar things together, such as attending sporting events or going to the park. Help him collect things to begin another scrapbook about his new home. Invite a family over for a meal with children around his age. Let him call or email old friends to ease the transition.

Appreciate the change. Erika, a veteran "mover" since childhood, shares that a move can create "an uprooted feeling that you don't really belong anywhere." However, she also feels that moving offers the opportunity to get to know a variety of wonderful people in many different places. Learning to appreciate the landscape and culture of various parts of the country is an additional benefit. Erika learned to enjoy the new and different instead of considering it strange or backward. Erika says that "It's the people, not the place that make home 'home.'"

Make positive memories by planning ahead. Erika encourages movers to plan ahead as much as possible, in anticipation of the move to avoid last minute stress. Make the move a lasting memory for the family by stopping to enjoy selected sights along the way. Don't forget to capture some of those prized moments on Kodak!

Ask for help. Erika further suggests that household boxes should be labeled according to content and destination. Have someone from outside help if possible, as much for peacekeeping as anything else. Erika comments, "Nothing brings the worst out in us like moving. My husband, Michael, and I were able to stay much calmer with my brother, Melvin, and my Dad around to help with the packing and driving."

Pace yourself when adjusting to new challenges. After two years in the States, Bob and Kim urge movers to have realistic expectations when handling new situations. They not only moved to a totally new country, but also to new roles as pastor and wife. Adapting to new terminology and regional dialect and culture has been a challenge. They have been forced to make adjustments in regard to America's healthcare and social security systems. The kids had to take driver's education all over again. Their daughter, who only needed two additional courses for high school graduation, was required to take a full course load her last year. Simply establishing credit, something we Americans take for granted, was a major obstacle in their establishment in the States. With all the red-tape and paperwork required upon entering a new country, Bob and Kim knew they would have to pace themselves, tackling one new item on their list each day. Otherwise, the many adjustments would be overwhelming.

Rely on God. Both Bob and Kim left good-paying jobs, a nice home, and good lifestyle to follow God's leading to America. They have had to rely on God to supply their every need. Digging deeper into God's Word, and spending more time in prayer hold more significance to them now. Possessions aren't nearly as important as they once thought.

Allow God to use you in your new place. Bob and Kim encourage other movers to be alert to ways God wants to use you in the lives of others. Think about what you have learned from your move, and how you can help others making a move. Bob and Kim feel they are now more sensitive to others going through change—a valuable asset when ministering to others. They believe the experience has taught them to depend more on God and less on themselves. The spiritual gains they have received from the move have outweighed any losses incurred. They gladly give God all the glory for His specific leading and direction in their lives!

If God has led you to move, dear reader, make it the best move ever! And if you have just moved to our area—hey, drop on by for some coffee or tea! We'd love to make a new friend.

Chapter Seven

When Abuse Strikes: The Silent Grief

*Anger will hold you prisoner;
forgiveness will set you free.*

I don't talk. I don't trust anybody. No one dare suspect. Guilt. Shame. Confusion. Betrayal. Helplessness. Worthlessness. Frustration. Fear. Anger. These are the emotions hiding within me.

Dare I feel? The pain is too intense. Perhaps, if I bury these horrible feelings, they will go away. I remain frozen, numb, unfeeling, unmoved. I cannot relive the cruel past. I dare not anticipate the future. I am locked into this present agony, the same harsh reality day after day after day. Is there no place to run, to hide, to escape my life? I cry into my pillow every night, but no one hears. No one cares.

I am the abused one. My loss is great. My grief runs deep.

Portrait of the Abuse Victim

Abuse represents something being taken away either physically, emotionally, or mentally resulting in a loss of safety, security, stability, control, and personal identity.

The abuse victim suffers isolation. He hesitates to tell anyone about the abuse for fear he will get into trouble. If the perpetrator is a family member or "friend," the victim may try to protect him. He may also try to protect other family members if the abuser has threatened to harm them if he tells.

Sexual abuse is especially damaging to a young child who is forced into the adult world before it is time. The child suffers a loss of innocence. While there is an increasing amount of male abuse, the majority of abuse victims are female. The abuse distorts her view of adults as trusting caregivers. If the abuser is her father, she is often confused about the role she plays within the family. In the morning, she is daddy's little girl and at night, his sex partner. She loves her dad and wants desperately to believe that he is good, all the while believing that she is terribly bad and did something to warrant the abuse. Her lost childhood impacts her deeply, for it is a time when her view of the world and adults is being formed. She is vulnerable emotionally, as well as physically. "Daddy is bigger than I am and is supposed to be smarter." The abuse causes a black cloud to hover over her life on into adulthood. She learns not to trust anyone. She struggles to control everybody and every aspect of her life, to somehow regain the control she lost as a youth.

Portrait of the Perpetrator

Most perpetrators are male and, in more cases than not, someone the victim knows. Often, the offender abuses in the same way he was abused as a child, and as a result, he, too, is filled with shame, hopelessness, and despair. He doesn't know how to relieve his emotional pain, so he repeats what he knows and has experienced. For example, a child who grows up receiving blood-producing beatings for no legitimate reason, believes that the abuse is normal, until he interacts with others outside his family, and discovers that not everyone has had the same experience.

Seeking acceptance, power, and control, the abuser unleashes his unprincipled behavior on the most vulnerable, usually a child or female of any age. Many times, he feels a child will accept him more readily than an adult will. Because he has been the recipient of abusive behavior himself, his buried anger brews into hatred which is then acted out on those physically closest to him. This only leads to further guilt.

Lies the Victim Believes and the Truth She Needs to Embrace

I deserved the abuse.

The truth is the sole responsibility lies in the lap of the offender. He is accountable for his own actions. Because she is created in the image of God, the abuse victim is a highly valued person and precious in the sight of her Maker (Ps. 139)—and so is the offender, by the way.

I did something to cause the abuse.

Often, a girl will feel that she brought on the abuse because she exuded sex appeal or some other behavior, warranting abuse. Often, her belief system is influenced by what the perpetrator has told her. For example, a father sexually abusing his daughter, may tell her he is teaching her how to relate to men. *The truth is the victim did not bring on the abuse.* Although high testosterone levels may trigger sexual abuse, most often the abuse is a ploy for power and control. Again, the responsibility is solely in the hands of the perpetrator.

I am bad.

Feelings of shame run so deep that they distort the victim's belief system about who she really is. In the case of sexual abuse, the victim may feel she is dirty or warped for feeling pleasure during sexual abuse. *The truth is the body is programmed to respond to certain stimuli. False guilt may cause her to blame herself for what the perpetrator did. She did not ask for the abuse nor did she initiate it. The abuser did.*

I can never be free.

Satan delights to hold the abuse victim in the grip of false guilt, anger, anxiety, bitterness, rejection, and unforgiveness. *The truth is God wants to release the chains of bondage and set the victim free!* That is the very reason He sent His only begotten Son into the world to suffer at the hands of His abusers on the cross. He shed His own precious blood in order to secure our forgiveness for all time and eternity. Jesus bore our griefs on the cross and He carried our sorrows. He endured the agony for our well-being (Isa. 53:4-6). We simply come to Him, and lay our garbage at the foot of His cross, and He takes care of the rest, as we build an altar out of our pain (Rom. 12:1-2). We will discuss this further in part six.

When we receive His free gift of forgiveness, we are delivered from the past. We can apply godly statements to our lives in the form of biblical self-talk. Search the Scriptures. The book of Ephesians is a wonderful place to begin uncovering the treasure of who you are in Christ. Our book, *Marriage With an Attitude*, contains a comprehensive listing of biblical "I am" statements, with Scripture references. Below are a few.

I am fearfully and wonderfully made (Ps. 139:14).

I am loved and valued by God (Jer. 31:3).

I am completely forgiven by God and totally accepted by Him (Eph. 1:7).

I am a brand new creation in Christ (2 Cor. 5:17).

I am set free (John 8:31-32).[1]

Seeing Abuse as God Sees It

When an abused person finally reaches the place where she can expose her buried feelings, she may express anger toward God. She may wonder, *If God is so big and so great and in control of everything, why didn't He stop my abuse?*

The truth is God did not cause the abuse. The perpetrator did. Through an act of His divine love, God created each one of us with a free will. We each have the God-given ability to choose Him and His goodness, or to choose evil and the resulting behavior. This biblical principle takes us all the way back to the Garden of Eden, where Adam and Eve made the choice to eat the forbidden fruit, incurring judgment on mankind. God doesn't keep evil from happening any more than He forces righteousness to happen.

God does, however, take the awful effects of abuse and turn them around for good to those who offer the twisted mess to Him. This is beautifully illustrated in Genesis 50:20 where Joseph responds to his jealous and abusive brothers after selling him into Egypt. He not only became a slave in a foreign land, but he was falsely accused of sexual misconduct, and unjustly thrown into prison. Joseph may have wondered, *Where is God in all of this?*

Joseph's response to his brothers is simply, "And as for you, you meant evil against me, but God meant it for good in order to bring about this present result, to preserve many people alive." Acts 7:9 says that, "God was with Joseph." God had delivered him out of prison and elevated him to a high position in the Egyptian government, using his skills to save the people from a devastating famine. Ultimately, he saved his own family—the very brothers who had abused him—from the same dreadful famine.

The most important step Joseph took in dealing with his abuse was to offer forgiveness to his brothers. He was only able to do this because he recognized God's hand in the whole situation. His brothers were astounded! They thought for sure he would retaliate and use the power of his position to imprison them or kill them. But not so. Joseph had received comfort from God and was able to extend that same comfort to his brothers.

God's ways are indeed mysterious! But when we entrust our lives to His keeping, He promises to turn our sorrows into joy.

The life and testimony of Corrie ten Boom is another remarkable illustration of the way God can bring healing into the life of an abuse victim. Taken captive for hiding Jews during World War II and trucked off to a prison camp, she was later released as the result of a clerical error. The following story, taken from *Guideposts Magazine,* touches any abuse scenario with the power of forgiveness.

I'm Still Learning to Forgive

It was in a church in Munich where I was speaking in 1947 that I saw him—a balding heavyset man in a gray overcoat, a brown felt hat clutched between his hands. One moment I saw the overcoat and the brown hat, the next, a blue uniform and a visored cap with its skull and crossbones.

Memories of the concentration camp came back with a rush: the huge room with its harsh overhead lights, the pathetic pile of dresses and shoes in the center of the floor, the shame of walking naked past this man. I could see my sister's frail form ahead of me, ribs sharp beneath the parchment of skin.

Betsie and I had been arrested for concealing Jews in our home during the Nazi occupation of Holland. This man had been a guard at Ravensbruck concentration camp where we were sent.

Now he was in front of me, hand thrust out: "A fine message, fraulein! How good it is to know that, as you say, all our sins are at the bottom of the sea!"

It was the first time since my release that I had been face to face with one of my captors and my blood seemed to freeze.

"You mentioned Ravensbruck in your talk," he was saying. "I was a guard there. But since that time," he went on, "I have become a Christian. I know that God has forgiven me for the cruel things I did there, but I would like to hear it from your lips as well. Fraulein"—again the hand came out—"will you forgive me?"

And I stood there—and could not. Betsie had died in that place—could he erase her slow terrible death simply for the asking?

It could not have been many seconds that he stood there, hand held out, but to me it seemed hours as I wrestled with the most difficult thing I had ever had to do.

For I had to do it—I knew that. The message that God forgives has a prior condition: that we forgive those who have injured us. "If you do not forgive men their trespasses," Jesus says, "neither will your Father in Heaven forgive your trespasses."

Still I stood there with the coldness clutching my heart. But forgiveness is an act of the will, and the will can function regardless of the temperature of the heart. "Jesus, help me!" I prayed silently. "I can lift my hand. I can do that much. You supply the feeling."

And so woodenly, mechanically, I thrust my hand into the one stretched out to me. And as I did, an incredible thing took place. The current started in my shoulder, raced down my arm, sprang into our joined hands. And then this healing warmth seemed to flood my whole being, bringing tears to my eyes.

"I forgive you, brother!" I cried. "With all my heart!"

For a long moment we grasped each other's hands, the former guard and former prisoner. I had never known God's love so intensely as I did then.[2]

You had no choice in your abuse, dear friend, but you do have a choice about whether you forgive your abuser and open the door for healing yourself. As Loren Fischer once said, "The difference between holding on to a hurt or releasing it with forgiveness—is like the difference between laying your head down at night on a pillow filled with thorns or a pillow filled with rose petals."

Help, Where Do I Turn?

You are ready to admit the truth about your abuse. Now you need help. Perhaps you need to literally get out of the situation you are in and seek a safe refuge. Check the phone book or call information for the nearest abuse hotline, an abuse shelter, or call 911 if in immediate danger. Talk to a counselor about your abuse and related feelings. It will take time to establish trust, but by all means, keep talking. Vent your feelings verbally and in writing. Work with the authorities to prosecute the offender. This may be extremely difficult and painful for you, but a necessary step to guard against further hurt to other innocent victims.

For long term therapy in dealing with your abuse, seek out a Christian counselor or someone trained in abuse issues. Jan Morrison, an abuse victim herself, directs a ministry solely devoted to the needs of the abused. Her non-profit service organization is especially geared towards adolescent victims and survivors of sexual abuse. You can contact her at the following address: Tree of Rest, Inc. P.O. Box 6167, Evanston, Illinois 60204 or call toll-free: 1-800-782-9834.

When Abuse Strikes: The Silent Grief

My work with Total Life Counseling brings me in contact with many abuse victims on a regular basis. One woman came to us through the help of a friend. She was suicidal when we placed her in our day treatment program. She shares the following account:

> I know that if I had not started the program on Friday, I would not have made it through the weekend. I had lots of doubts that it was going to work, but I'm glad I didn't give up. The counselors began teaching me that I needed to go through a process of healing.
>
> The first thing I had to do was tell myself the truth about my abuse. I had to face what had happened to me and distinguish between true guilt and false guilt. I always felt I deserved what was happening to me because I never told anyone. False guilt. True guilt lies on the man who was abusing me.
>
> The second part of the healing process is the hardest, and that part is forgiveness. I had to choose to forgive and I also had to choose to receive forgiveness. I honestly don't know which was harder for me to do—choose to forgive someone who had done such awful things to me that they almost destroyed my life or receive God's forgiveness for all the sins I had committed.
>
> It was very difficult to go through all this by myself, but one morning while I was outside, I sat down on the sidewalk and began talking to God. I told Him how lonely I was, that I just needed someone to be with me. I don't know how to explain what happened next, but as I sat there, I felt an awesome presence.
>
> I felt that if I turned my head, I could see Jesus right there sitting beside me. I was overcome with a feeling of comfort that my God and Savior was right there saying to

me, "It's all right, you're not alone. I'm here with you and I'm not going to leave you."

After that day, my life changed, and I began to find my way out of all my misery. By the fifth day into the day treatment program at Total Life, I had a major breakthrough.

We were doing one of our exercises and I found out how sexual abuse can lead to joy and happiness. I know that sounds very strange, but let me explain.

Based on the sexual abuse, I believed my abuser changed the person I would have become. I was angry about that. Total Life offered verses to counter that belief. The story of Joseph in Genesis 50:20 offered me hope. Knowing "that God causes **all things** to work together for good to those who love God, to those who are called according to His purpose" (Rom. 8:28, emphasis added) offered me power. Philippians 4:11 offered me contentment.

Now when you have hope, power, and contentment, how can you not have joy in your life? Regardless of all the stuff in my life, God is enough! I thank God for giving me back my life and allowing me to be here today.

If you need help dealing with abuse, Total Life Counseling would be pleased to assist you. Located at 5401 Fallowater Ln. #C, Roanoke, Virginia 24014, you can call us at (540) 989-1383.

Often, we recommend that clients write a letter to their abuser, to God, and to anyone else they have strong feelings toward in relation to the abuse. The letter serves to get feelings out. It is not necessarily sent.

As we close this chapter, we offer a letter to you from God. We want you to know that God does understand your heartache and offers you hope and deliverance from your grief.

When Abuse Strikes: The Silent Grief

A Letter from God to the Abuse Victim

(Supply your name after the salutation. Place the offender's name on the blank lines.)

Dear _____,

My dear, precious child. I love you more than you realize. Although you were not aware at the time of your abuse, in that moment, when you felt so alone and so used, I was there. I was weeping as I saw what _____ did to you.

You thought about Me. You wondered on that day and the days that followed why I didn't step in and stop the abuse. You were angry with me. You struggled with your feelings. You felt betrayed by Me.

My precious _____, I don't cause abuse. I created _____ with a free will. I don't keep evil from happening any more than I force righteousness to happen. Each individual is created with the ability to choose. That is love. I am Love, so I cannot operate out of anything but love.

On those days when you thought you could not get out of bed and go to school, but you did anyway, I helped you.

During those times when you felt like everyone knew, when you wanted desperately to run away and hide, I felt your shame. I tried to remind you who you truly are, that you are made in My image and a highly valued person in my sight.

My Son suffered beyond comprehension to prove My love for you and to secure you to Myself forever. I give you permission to cry, to stop feeling guilty for what happened. It was not your fault. I give you permission to love yourself because I love you. I want you to forgive yourself and _____ for I have already made provision for your forgiveness through the shed blood of My Son on the cross. His death, burial, and resurrection bring you new life if you will only receive it.

The choice is yours. I hope you will come to Me. I am waiting.

Love,

GOD

Chapter Eight

Miscarriage: The Misunderstood Loss

A miscarriage is a sudden, unexpected, and shocking loss of life. It shatters your hopes for children and fills you with doubts about the future… it is normal to have many strong and unpleasant emotions associated with it.
~Hank Pizer and Christine O-Brien Palinski~
authors of *Coping with a Miscarriage*

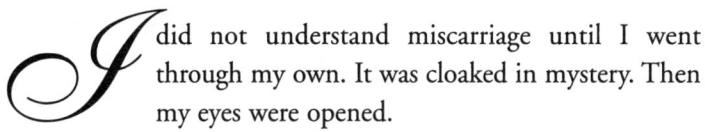

I did not understand miscarriage until I went through my own. It was cloaked in mystery. Then my eyes were opened.

Three years after our second daughter was born, I was pregnant again and sick as a dog. Two other friends had just delivered babies and were trying to encourage me to *hang in there*—my turn was coming. But at twelve weeks gestation, all I could see was the long road ahead, struggling day after day to drag myself out of bed, care for my family, throw-up, and drag myself back to bed. I felt terrible, life seemed bleak, and as far as I was concerned, my misery was here to stay. I took my fluctuating emotions to God, praying, "Oh Father, give me the grace to cope with this pregnancy, to take one day at a time, and to release my anxieties into Your loving care."

A month later and feeling somewhat better, our world suddenly came crashing down around us when Chuck returned to work on the Monday after Easter to discover he no longer had a job. After five years as an academic counselor at the university level, financial cutbacks necessitated his layoff. The following Thursday, we piled boxes into the car and drove to school to clear out his office. With tears, shock, and disbelief, we silently rambled about the room gathering items and placing them in a box. With boxes sealed and memories safely tucked inside, we drove home in silence, each conversing with God in his own way in the privacy of his own heart.

❧

Two weeks later, a new opportunity opened up for Chuck through the prompting of a friend who was going to train to sell life insurance. Chuck had also applied for a position as a psychologist at a local facility for the mentally challenged, but had not heard back from them. After prayer and thought, he decided to proceed with the two-week insurance training in Richmond, Virginia—a three-hour trip from our home. The Lord was reassuring us that He would accomplish all things for us.

Since I was in my fourth month—an uncertain time in my pregnancy, for I had lost our second baby at that same time—Chuck urged me to call my parents to come and stay with me and the girls during his two-week absence. I dismissed the idea as unnecessary and sent him off to Richmond. Though I missed him greatly, I was occupied with Rachel and Michelle, the house, and, of course—my coming baby.

A week and a half passed. All was well, until Wednesday evening. Chuck was due home that Friday after his final exam. I woke up during the night with mild contractions and some spotting. Alone in my room in our spacious queen-sized bed, I prayed that God would take control of my rampant emotions, that He would guard my heart and mind, and protect my little baby from harm. I did not want to think of losing another child. I tried to stay calm and in control. I knew six-year-old Rachel and three-year-old Michelle were sleeping in the next room. They would be full of energy the next day. They would need me. I had to keep a level head for them. I tried to sleep, but all I accomplished was a few brief naps, always waking to the sound of the numbers on our clock clicking over to another minute. *Had it only been a half hour since I closed my eyes?* I groaned. The night crept on and, finally, the morning light dawned through our bedroom window.

I heard the girls moving about in their room and knew they would burst through my bedroom door at any moment. I had the wee hours of the night to formulate a plan, so I busied myself to execute that plan. I wearily threw on some clothes and left the room to tend to Rachel and Michelle. While I helped Michelle dress, I explained to them that I needed to go to the doctor for a checkup and that they would get to play with some friends for awhile. Several phone calls later and still no sitter, I decided to put the girls in our station wagon and head for our old house in another part of town, in hopes that Terri would be home. She and her husband had two young boys and had purchased our home a year earlier.

Pulling up to our former home and escorting our girls up the long flight of black steps, brought back memories—some pleasant and some not so pleasant—but I did not have the stamina to reflect very long on either. I was too absorbed in the requirements of the moment. Terri answered the door with her usual cheery greeting. She heartily agreed to watch the girls while I went to the doctor. Relieved that I had finally found a sitter, I relaxed in the knowledge that Rachel and Michelle were in good hands. Still numb from lack of sleep, I turned to go. A soft April rain was falling. I hurried as best I could to the car.

Dr. Hall was out of town—never a good sign—so I was scheduled to see a female obstetrician, which was a new experience for me. She turned out to be quite pleasant and efficient. Determining that I had a bladder infection, she prescribed some medicine and sent me home to rest.

The rain was still falling when I pulled up to the pharmacy. The temperature seemed colder. I shuddered as I clumsily clutched at my sweater and made a dash for the store entrance. By now I was feeling pretty sorry for myself. I was all alone. No one in the world knew how wretched I felt at that moment. No one, except God.

Back home again, I called Terri to update her on my condition. She insisted on keeping the girls for the night. I didn't argue. I hung up the receiver, took my medicine, put on my nightgown, and curled up in bed for a long nap.

I woke up three hours later and decided to call my friend, Sylvia. I knew I needed to confide in someone. She listened, comforted, and encouraged. She was just as supportive now as she had been years earlier when we lost our little son. As I hung up the receiver, I remembered how I had called her on the phone the day after our son died.

Sylvia was no stranger to grief and loss. On that sad day for me, she shared how God had given her a special verse in Psalms (56:8) that had been a comfort to her after her mother lost her extended battle with cancer. Sylvia told me over the phone, "You know, Eileen, God puts your tears in His bottle and writes them down in His book. That's how precious your tears are to God." She had done one of the nicest things a friend can do when another friend is hurting—she had given me permission to cry, to release my feelings to God, to let go of the grief inside. She reminded me then, as she had today, that God cares, that He is intimately acquainted with all my ways, including my deep feelings of sadness and pain.

An hour passed. As I lay watching the evening news, I heard the doorbell ring. "Who in the world could that be?" I questioned out loud. Curious, I grabbed my robe and crept downstairs to answer the front door. As I pulled open the door, there to my surprise and delight stood Sylvia with two Burger King sacks, a liter of soda, and six pink carnations arranged in a vase.

"Thought you might like some company for supper," Sylvia quipped, grinning with that mischievous smile so characteristic of my friend.

I quickly replied, "Come on in. This is great. What a treat!"

We unpacked our burgers, poured some drinks, and headed back upstairs to my bedroom to chow-down on the goodies. I placed my beautiful carnations on the night stand by my bed where I could thoroughly soak them in. As I stepped back to admire them, I thought it odd that four of the carnations were grouped together, one was off to itself, and still another was merely a bud. I commented to Sylvia how the flowers reminded me of my family— four here on earth together, one already in heaven, and still another yet to bloom, whether on earth or in heaven, I did not yet know. After supper, we lay on the bed chatting for awhile. She encouraged me to call Chuck that evening, but I assured her that he was planning to call and check in with me anyway. As she picked up her purse to leave, she firmly instructed me, in her matronly manner, to call her if I needed anything at all. At this point, I was more than glad to oblige and felt relieved that I had her support.

For the next two hours, I nodded off and on as the television droned in the background. At last, the phone rang. I lifted the receiver and heard Chuck's voice on the other end. I wanted to either yank him through the phone or crawl through the phone to him. I knew I could do neither, so solaced myself with the sound of his voice.

"How are you doing?" he inquired.

I took a deep breath and shared the events of the day. He responded with obvious concern. "Do you want me to come home? I'll come right now, if you need me to."

I knew he could do nothing for me. I also knew he had a final exam to take the next day for his insurance training. He would travel home right after the exam. I would see him tomorrow. "No, don't come home," I replied. "I'll take my medicine and rest. I'm sure this will clear up. The girls are cared for and you will be home tomorrow anyway. I'll be fine." We said our goodbyes, hung up the phone, and I fell asleep.

I woke up Friday morning with stronger contractions. I glanced at the clock on our night stand. The big, bold, white numbers glared at me—1:30 a.m. I tried in vain to deny the contractions, to pretend I was dreaming, but the betraying sensations only intensified. I turned on the light and lay back on my pillow to pray. "Oh, Father, this can't be happening again. Please don't let me lose this baby, too. Please help me to relax. Maybe these contractions will go away."

The contractions were still strong at 4:30 a.m., so I decided to call Sylvia for a ride to the hospital. She arrived in fifteen minutes and met me at the door, where I was taping up a message for Chuck. As I closed the storm door and walked down our sidewalk, I glanced back at the house and grieved that Chuck would have to discover the news in such a cold, impersonal way. As Sylvia and I took our seats in the car and hooked our seat belts, I murmured, "I never imagined that I would lose another baby."

Miscarriage: The Misunderstood Loss

The maternity staff promptly put me to bed and began monitoring my progress. Dr. Hall was still on vacation in Bermuda, so I was greeted by the female obstetrician that had examined me the day before. I was glad that she was on call and not a total stranger. She seemed to have a sensitivity about her that only another woman could exhibit. I could tell by her determination to help that she was prepared to do everything she possibly could for me and my unborn child. She was eager for me to call Chuck, but I knew he was preparing for his exam. I did not want to upset him. Besides, he would have to get a ride home and that would take at least three hours. "No," I insisted. "Things are better off this way. There is nothing he can do to save our baby. God is in control of that."

Sylvia stayed by my side, praying and encouraging. The doctor decided to give me a muscle relaxant which began to take effect around 10:30 a.m. As I drifted into "lah-lah" land, I began to see lizards crawling over each other on the ceiling. In my dazed condition, I thought I was seeing a television image reflected from someone else's room. In actuality, I was in an enclosed room, but in my confusion, I concocted this explanation for the lizard vision. By 11:45 a.m., my condition had worsened and the doctor, nurse, and I prepared for the inevitable—the delivery of my premature child. With resolve to spare Sylvia the sight of my tiny, dead baby, and an inner need to experience the delivery on my own, I asked Sylvia to leave the room.

Ten minutes later, with a gentle push, I delivered our fragile baby girl.

"She's still breathing," the doctor calmly stated.

"Is she in any pain?" I managed to ask.

"No," replied the doctor. "She will simply fall asleep....Do you want to hold her?" she asked.

"Yes," I mumbled.

Through tear-filled eyes, I watched as the doctor carefully

wrapped my baby girl in a blanket—so different from my previous experience with our little son. Here was another woman, not a doctor, identifying with my need to mother my child in her last moments. She handed me the bundle and I held the tiny package for a minute. She was gone and I knew it. I felt detached. Somehow, holding her seemed meaningless, almost morbid. I handed my bundle to the nurse and she carried it out the door. A few seconds later, Sylvia opened the door and approached my bedside. She took my hand and said nothing. On the threshold of grief, words are empty. My friend knew that. After a while, Sylvia left to rejoin her husband and two children, and I can only suppose, to regain her equilibrium. The day had been a tremendous strain for her, I'm sure, and it was time to rest in the comfort of her own family.

The orderlies arrived and wheeled me down the hall to another room, where I would stay for the night. Riding past the squalling babies in the nursery made my loss more intense. As we approached my room, I turned my head as the orderlies maneuvered the gurney to get inside the door. I couldn't help noticing the sign on my neighbor's door—*It's a Girl!* That did it. I covered my face with my hands and sobbed.

I was alone. As far as I knew, no one else but Sylvia and Terri knew about the day's happenings. In some ways, I was ready to be alone, although I anxiously longed for Chuck to break through the door, and hold me, and share in our joint loss. I rested, ate, rested some more, and called the house several times with no answer. By now, the time was 9:30 p.m. At last, Chuck bolted through my door, and, with what seemed like one desperate leap, landed by my bedside. Without any words, he grabbed me and held me for some time. We hugged so hard. We cried and talked, and then made plans for the next day.

The next day came. I felt as if it never would, but it did. To my great relief, Chuck finally arrived at the hospital to take me home. I knew the next few weeks were going to be difficult, but one truth I had learned from our previous miscarriage, was that God was with me and He would never leave me nor forsake me (Heb. 13:5b).

Arriving home, I climbed the stairs to our bedroom and surveyed the room. *Was it only yesterday that I had left for the hospital?* I mused. *It seemed like an eternity ago.* I glanced at the vase of carnations on the night stand. I noticed that the one solitary bud was now in full bloom. My heart leaped as I considered the sweet picture the flower represented of my little girl in full blossom in her heavenly home. Though I was not home to see the bud open, I imagined that at noon on Friday, April 18, 1986, the petals burst forth in celebration of my baby's entrance into heaven to enjoy her heavenly Father forever and ever. Our little girl, born too soon for our liking, was born at just the right time according to God's timetable. He must have yearned for another star to shine in the heavenlies.

Thus, little sister joined big brother. I could imagine their happy faces as they met and climbed onto Jesus' lap to view His beaming, compassionate face. I could hear His words to the annoyed disciples, "Let the children alone, and do not hinder them from coming to Me; for the kingdom of heaven belongs to such as these" (Matt. 19:14).

As I stood there as if in a dream, I decided to get my journal and write a letter to our baby girl.

Dear Little One,

Mommy and Daddy love you so much and always will. Our aching hearts cannot begin to equal the love that our dear Savior has for you. How much better you understand that than we do, since you are with Him now. You are one of the special few chosen to view the Lord's face without ever having to taste of this world's evil.

A pink carnation began to bloom for you today, for indeed this is your coronation day, your crowning moment. We've said our earthly goodbyes, but one day, we will say our heavenly hellos, and enter into everlasting life together.

We love you and miss you. We will never forget that God allowed you to be ours for a time, however brief. There will always be a place in our hearts where you are. The knowledge that you are with Jesus will keep us until we see you again.

Goodbye our sweet child.

Love,

Mommy and Daddy

As I finished my letter, Rachel and Michelle bounced into the room to hug me and smother me with childish kisses—exactly what I needed at that moment. God reminded me that He had lavished me with many blessings. Yes, He had pulled the bus up to my front door and carted away some precious cargo, but right there, right then, He was releasing His love to me through my two earthly daughters, who had more than enough love to go around.

Over the next several weeks, He would continue to teach me that, yes, He gives and yes, He takes away. My job was to bless His name in the midst of the trial, even though with my limited perspective, I could not understand all of His dealings. Like Job of old, God desired that my growth in Him transcend to a new level of total abandonment to His will. I could see from searching through Scripture that God was trying to fashion me into a better minister of comfort to other hurting people. Chuck testified to the same in his own life. Since that time, he has shared our loss with many clients at Total Life Counseling.

Sharing our miscarriages with counselees doesn't mean I know exactly how they feel in their particular loss. But it does help them see that they are not talking to a cold, stoic clinician. I have lost, too. I am a card carrying member of the human race. Unearthing my reality often helps them open up and share their loss, too. They realize their grief is not silly or meaningless. It's real.

Misconceptions About Miscarriage

Often miscarriage is a misunderstood event. Because the medical profession still does not fully know why miscarriages occur, the loss is shrouded in mystery. The woman may succumb to several misconceptions surrounding her miscarriage.

I did something to cause the miscarriage.

Guilt is a common feeling among women who have miscarried. They tend to blame themselves for the event. If only I hadn't lifted that heavy box or painted the bedroom. If only I had eaten more vegetables. If only I hadn't jogged on Wednesday, this would not have happened. *The truth is, in the majority of cases, the miscarriage or spontaneous abortion was beyond the woman's control.* Her body expelled the baby because there was either an abnormality in the fetus, her uterus was malformed, an infection was present, or a host of other reasons the medical profession has not yet discovered. Blaming herself will only keep her stuck in the past and prolong her grieving.

I am a failure.

A woman often suffers a lowered self-image due to her thoughts regarding the miscarriage. She mistakenly feels that she failed herself because of certain expectations she has concerning the pregnancy and motherhood in general. She feels she has failed her husband and family. This, of course, is untrue as she had no control over the response of her body. She may fear future pregnancies because she is uncertain as to how her body will react. She feels out of control.

Once the miscarriage is over, I can get on with life as usual.

I tried to do this after our first miscarriage, picking up with my housework and daily responsibilities as if nothing had happened. Underlying feelings of anger and sadness kept churning within me, affecting my relationship with Chuck, until months later I finally spewed them out before the Lord, which opened the door to my emotional healing.

A woman needs to grieve her loss fully. Often the losses that occur suddenly, with no warning, as with a miscarriage, are the hardest to deal with. She needs to talk her feelings out with God in prayer and in writing. She also needs to share her feelings with her husband and with a trusted friend. Sometimes, another woman who has had a similar experience can be of help and comfort.

A man does not feel any pain associated with the loss.

A woman needs to recognize that her husband is grieving in his own way, too. He may be hesitant to express his feelings, because he feels the need to be strong for his wife and keep the function of work and home going while she is recovering. During our first miscarriage, I was so absorbed in my own pain that I did not see Chuck's hurt. I even vented my anger on him, accusing him of not feeling the loss or caring about the baby. In truth, he was hurting, too. Since he was not physically attached to the baby as I was, he could not fully relate to the empty feeling of losing a part of himself. First, he grieved for my hurt and pain. Secondly, he grieved the loss of our child.

I (Chuck) shielded my feelings from Eileen in hopes of easing her discomfort when, in actuality, I needed to face the pain honestly and talk through the feelings with her. Honest sharing would eliminate the distance between us, pulling us together as we worked through a common grief. Since I lost my job two weeks before our second miscarriage, our grief was compounded. We had two major losses to grieve. As a man, my role as provider was threatened, which affected my significance. I was busy re-establishing my identity when we were side-swiped by the miscarriage. When I saw Eileen in such physical pain at the hospital, I felt powerless and helpless. I was afraid she might die. There was nothing I could do but tell her I loved her and pray for her and the baby. Once she was home from the hospital, I had to keep the household machinery running while she recovered physically and emotionally. I couldn't give myself permission to fully grieve until I met the needs of the family in front of me.

Sometimes, a man needlessly shoulders the responsibility for the miscarriage and goes overboard trying to make things up to his wife. While kind deeds are helpful, open sharing is even more healing after the loss. He needs to express his fears and doubts so that their future relationship together will not be hampered. Sharing creates strength in the marriage and acts like a glue, bonding the couple together. Eileen and I have found that writing our thoughts and feelings down is an effective way of expressing grief when emotions are fresh and unrefined.

Reestablishing Your Life After a Miscarriage

Understand that grieving the loss of your baby will take time. Your miscarriage experience was different from any other woman, yet you share a common bond with those who have lost babies. Find a friend to share with.

Realize that many well-meaning people will not understand your loss. They may try to minimize your pain with statements like, "You're young, you'll have more children." That may be true, but on the heels of a miscarriage, the words sound insensitive and do not acknowledge the child you lost. Many do not even want to talk about the loss, but your feelings are still there and very real. Express them to someone who is genuinely concerned.

Accept the physical help of others, so that you have plenty of quiet time to sort out your feelings, and rest to recover emotionally and physically. Remember, your body is adjusting to hormonal changes just as it would after childbirth.

Plan a week-end retreat with your husband, a special meal, or an evening out to recover as a couple and renew your love and commitment to each other. Buy something just for yourself, like a new dress. I remember coming home from the hospital and opening the closet door. Maternity clothes that I had already begun to wear lined the rack. My time in them had been cut short because of the miscarriage. I had to grieve something as simple, yet as real as that.

If you have other children, receive their love. Resist the temptation to push them away. They are full of affection and also questions about the baby. Answer them honestly and in terms they can understand, geared to their maturity level. Relieve the child's concern if you sense he blames himself in any way for the miscarriage. He may be thinking, *If I had let mommy rest that day, this would not have happened* or, *If I had picked up my toys like mommy asked me to, this would not have happened.* The fact is everyone surrounding the loss tends to blame himself in some way or another, but his thinking is irrational and untrue. No one is to blame for the miscarriage.

Be patient in planning another pregnancy. Give your body and mind a few months to recover. Ask God for His perfect timing. Seek medical advice if there is a pattern of miscarriage. Both your husband and you may need to undergo testing to determine the cause of the miscarriages and what potential treatment is required. Bathe any decisions concerning medical procedures in prayer together with your husband. Remember, you are a team. God will direct you as you turn your body and family over to Him.

Chapter Nine

Infertility: Empty Arms and Aching Hearts

> Coping with infertility requires the same kind of psychological and
> physical strength as does coping with the death of a parent,
> a divorce, or a life-threatening disease.
> ~RESOLVING INFERTILITY—THE NATIONAL INFERTILITY ASSOCIATION~

Equally as devastating as miscarriage is the crisis of infertility. Sometimes, the two accompany the couple as they board an emotional roller-coaster. Filled with anticipation, husband and wife hop on the ride, climb the hill, and crest the top, only to zoom to the bottom in disappointment. They jump onboard the next month and experience the same disappointing ride. Soon a pattern develops. Cherished plans crash into a heap of dashed hopes, squelched dreams, and despair. Feelings of worthlessness and guilt bubble to the surface. Both husband and wife may wonder, *What am I doing wrong?* Varying opinions by medical professionals foster further confusion. Fear takes root. The couple questions, *Will we ever be able to conceive?* Facing the prospect of remaining childless, the couple may turn on one another. Jealousy over other pregnant couples creeps in. Loss of purpose and meaning results.

An Age-Old Problem

Infertility is as old as time itself. Down through history, a woman's status was deeply entrenched in her reproductive ability. She sought her husband's favor by the number of children she could produce. The fertile wives often ridiculed the barren wife. Such was Hannah's case in 1 Samuel 1. According to the account, her husband, Elkanah, clearly loved her and agonized over her pain (vs. 5,8), but she would not be comforted. She longed for a son, but the Lord had closed her womb (vs. 5,6).

That the Lord is in charge of the womb is evident from other scriptural accounts as well. Childless Sarai tells Abraham in Genesis 16:2 that, "the Lord has prevented me from bearing children." Later, Isaac prays to the Lord on behalf of Rebekah in Genesis 25:21, and she conceives. On still another occasion, in Genesis 29:31-30:25, the sister-wife tag team (Rachel and Leah) acknowledge that God opened Leah's womb and closed Rachel's. Thus ensues a bitter contest employing the reproductive services of the sisters' maids to see who can bear Jacob the most babies. Jealousy. Rivalry. Conniving. Scheming. Negotiating. Manipulating. Exchanging mandrakes or "love apples" (sexual enhancers) for a night with Jacob. I wonder if Jacob felt tormented, frustrated, bewildered, or simply hunkered down and enjoyed the nightly ritual. He didn't seem to mind producing on command. You don't hear him complaining that "all she ever wants is my body!" Maybe he stayed stocked in Viagra. Perhaps, he stopped by the mandrake field on his way home from work to grab a few extra mandrakes for himself, just to be on the safe side. Whatever the case, he played the mating game well, resulting in twelve sons and one daughter among the four women.

Equipped for Motherhood

God has equipped a woman physically and emotionally to be a mother. Even in today's world with increased focus on careers, a woman's heartbeat thumps with longing to nurture a child. In her desperate desire, Hannah took her pain to the Lord (1 Sam. 1:10). She did not conceal her grief. She wept. She responded to her loss with fervent prayer. I wonder if she would have prayed so intensely had she not believed God was the giver of life. Hannah actively pursued God with her grief, rather than passively pine away in her circumstances. Her prayer ultimately gave birth to peace and praise over God's answer—a baby son!

Viewing Infertility as a Loss

With the rising tide of infertility sweeping the nation, barren couples feel the loss intensely. They not only lose control over their own bodies, but question their identity, often feeling they lose respect in the eyes of family and other fertile couples. They may go into hiding or immerse themselves in work to avoid confronting others who are expecting babies. Loneliness, envy, and depression clamor for attention. Feeling oppressed by the constant doctors' visits, meticulous timing of intercourse, medication, and temperature readings, the couple is frustrated at not being able to fulfill a basic human function. As a result, spouses may express anger toward one another, blame the other for the problem, or harass each other over sexual procedures, causing strain in the marriage. As with any loss, open, honest, loving communication of thoughts and feelings is crucial.

Because closure to infertility is so uncertain, couples may get stuck in the grieving cycle as they seek just one more medical breakthrough, wait just one more month, all the while hoping their quest will bear results. Thoughts pour in: *What if we never have a child? Can we live with that reality? When do we stop yearning for what we've tried years to attain?* At times, one hears of a couple who finally accepts their loss and then goes on to conceive. They finally relaxed and nature took its course.

Viewing Infertility as a Gift

At some point in the couple's journey, with the help of physicians, perhaps even an established support group, prayer, and consideration, husband and wife must choose to move on with their lives. They may realize that their loss opens the door to some possible gain. Checking into alternatives to biological parenthood, such as adoption, foster parenting, or involvement in other children's lives (nieces, nephews, church kids, community organizations), they discover a whole new world of nurturing opportunities. I've talked to teachers who lamented that they could never have a child of their own, but who lit up when they talked about the impact they've had in the lives of countless school children.

Some women gain such fulfillment from their careers that they do not view infertility as a significant loss, while other women do not find the same comfort from their professions. Certain couples adjust their thinking, and view the loss as more time to pursue their own interests, or invest energy in the lives of other children. None of these options removes the hurt of infertility nor minimizes the need to grieve the loss fully, but at some point in a healthy grieving process, the couple discovers ways to compensate for their loss. Dr. Albert Decker, an infertility specialist, reports that, "Many couples who came to realize that their union would remain barren, report that their marriage, in time, became particularly strong and satisfying. Some report that they live for one another, others enjoy indulging themselves, many somehow manage to put children, or young people, into their lives."[2] Ultimately, a couple who views infertility as God's will for their marriage is free to move on with their lives. They choose to turn their situation into a vehicle for good and godly service to others.

Brett and Linda's Story

Brett and Linda struggled with the challenge of infertility for over five years, when they decided that adoption was the path on

Infertility: Empty Arms and Aching Hearts

which God was leading them. Brett readily admits that trying to conceive was a trial, filled with much disappointment and grief, but one which he believes had a God-ordained purpose.

Early attempts to conceive, with no results, left both Brett and Linda frustrated over not being able to attain a goal they had come to expect as a married couple. Over time, Linda's frustration turned into anger, despair, and helplessness as she realized that she might never become pregnant. Linda says, "No matter how hard I tried, I couldn't make it happen. I was mad at God, but did not turn away from Him as I had in my earlier Christian walk when I didn't get my way." Although Linda fought with God, she always drew to Him for comfort. Prior loss issues had taught her to rely heavily on God. She was willing to trust Him with the infertility, clinging to Jeremiah 29:11 for strength: "'For I know the plans that I have for you,' declares the Lord, 'plans for welfare and not for calamity to give you a future and a hope.'"

Linda confesses that the desire for a family was extremely difficult to relinquish to God. Since every month brought renewed hope, Linda struggled to continually lay her desires at Jesus' feet. She reports that, "at the same time I was trying to relinquish, we were trying to get pregnant. It was like I had glue on my hands, as I tried desperately to submit my will to the Father."

Over time, Brett and Linda realized that what had been their dream was not God's dream for them. It was such a painful period in their lives. They still ache when they think about it. It was a huge loss, accompanied by a real period of grieving.

However, Linda shares that the Lord spoke directly to her when she was probably at her lowest point. She relates the following story.

One Saturday morning, I was talking on the phone with my mother who lives in Mississippi. Not wanting to worry her, I had never been transparent with Mother about the intensity of my pain, until today. I knew she was praying for us, but I simply could not shield my tears from her any longer. As I wept over the phone, I remember saying to her, "Mother, I've done everything I know to do…. I don't know what else I'm supposed to do… I just don't know what else I'm supposed to do…!"

The next day after church, Mother called me. I thought that was odd since we had just spoken the day before. She said she had something to share with me. That morning, Mother had gone to church as she always does and she was chatting with an old family friend, Irene, after Sunday School. Irene knew nothing about our struggle to have a family. That morning Irene asked about me. Mother said, "Well, it is funny that you would ask about Linda. She and her husband are really struggling to have a family and Linda is very sad." Irene then said, "I had a dream about Linda last night. She was very sad and tearful and kept saying, 'I've done everything I know to do…. I don't know what else I'm suppose to do…. I just don't know what else I'm supposed to do!' I said in the dream, 'Linda, just trust God, let go and trust God,' and then Linda said, 'Oh, I have and I will….'" And that was the end of Irene's dream.

Well, needless to say, I knew God had spoken to me. I knew He had not abandoned me. About a month after that incident with Irene, Brett and I began to tentatively get information on adoption. I say tentatively, because if birthing our family was not God's plan (and I had thought surely it was), then I thought that adopting our children might not be His plan either. Perhaps He wanted us childless for a reason only He knew. But as is always the case, when one gets on the same page with God, things begin to happen. And happen they did! Alec was in our arms within four months of our first adoption inquiry. The Lord obviously blew the doors wide open, and Brett and I both took that as affirmation that we were in the deep channels of His will.

Brett and Linda believe that God turned their loss into gain by providing them with the incredible privilege of experiencing adoption—not once, but twice! They share the following:

> Just as I am sure it is hard for others to put into words the birthing experience, it is hard for us to put into words the adoption experience. It reached far into the deepest level of our souls. Not to mention that the Lord blew the doors open for us—there was no obstacle anywhere. We didn't have the money, but the Lord sent us money. We thought we would have to wait forever, but we waited less than three months! Then, when we began pursuing our second adoption, the Lord did the same thing.
>
> We are the proud parents of two beautiful boys. I can't imagine them not being our sons. The Lord sent us many small confirmations along the way to let us know that He had always intended Alec and Clay to be our sons. For example, Brett and I, unknowingly, used the same names for our boys that both the birth mothers had used. Alec's birth mother had named him Taylor Alexander, we used Matthew Alec. Clay's birth mother had used Stephen John, we used Stephen Clay. There are tons of names out there. We don't think our choice was coincidental.
>
> I (Linda) must say that one of the enormous gains of being called to adoption is a deeply personal understanding that God has adopted me as His daughter. As a Christian, I had always understood that fact, but I never felt that fact with the intensity that I do now. I am the adopted daughter of God Almighty and nothing will ever sever that bond. Our boys will grow up understanding the incredible love involved in being adopted by their earthly parents, which only foreshadows a far greater love

beckoning them to the highest privilege as adopted sons of their heavenly Father.

Still, Brett and Linda admit that there have been adjustments along the way. "The major adjustment was aligning our way of thinking to God's way of thinking and moving," say Brett and Linda. "Once that process was finally done, we would have to say there has been no real adjusting at all regarding infertility. We simply moved forward in the incredible joy of having our two beautiful boys. However, we must say that the whole adoption experience almost seemed like an 'out of body' experience at times. Especially the day we brought Alec home, and, to a lesser extent, the day we brought Clay home. It was incredibly emotional and, indeed, miraculous, and yet so surrealistic," the couple concludes.

Linda shares that "looking back on our experience, I only wish I could have relinquished earlier. But as I said before, my hands had glue on them! However, in all honesty, I don't know if that was possible. It was a journey that we had to take to bring us to the crossroads to receive Alec and Clay. Had we gotten there earlier and pursued adoption earlier, neither Alec or Clay would have been there! I would relive every ounce of pain a hundred times over to be their mother."

Linda continues, "I encourage couples to remain steadfast in their trust in God. Yes, you are on an emotional roller coaster, but at the end of the day, always know that you are His child and He hasn't left you hanging in the wind. He *will* unfold His plan for you in His time. In your anger and frustration, always run to Him. He is your *only* comfort."

To those of you who may be considering adoption as an alternative to biological parenthood, I include the following letters written by Brett and Linda to the birth mother of their first adopted son. We pray you find them encouraging as you work through your own grieving process.

Dear Birth Mother,

It is with truly grateful hearts that Linda and I thank you for making our family possible. Your courage to deliver your baby and your sacrifice to place the child for adoption is matched by our resolve to be devoted parents and honor your act of love.

We have wanted a family for many years and have struggled for over five years through the burden of infertility. Although the journey has been filled with much disappointment and grief, we have known that we were on this path for a reason. With all our hearts, we both believe that there is a purpose to the circumstances in life and that God is working to make good out of both your circumstance and ours. God has brought you and Linda and me together at this juncture in our lives through feelings of despair and anguish to hope and promise.

I want to assure you that Linda and I are committed to our marriage and to one another. We have both had the good fortune to grow up in homes where the institution of marriage was honored and our parents respected and cherished one another. I sincerely believe it is a privilege to love my wife in a way that reflects a healthy example of marriage for our child.

I find myself very eager to begin experiencing fatherhood. In so many ways, I have been preparing for this role my entire life and am now filled with anticipation that the opportunity is drawing near. I have such fond memories of my own father as I was growing up. He took time with me, always there for a pick-up ballgame in the neighborhood with my friends; and he always let me know that he loved me. In recent years, I have had boyhood friends confide that as boys they often envied the relationship I had with "Pop." That close relationship continues to this day. As an adult, I have come to fully appreciate how seriously both my father and mother took their responsibilities as parents.

God has given me a real heart for fatherhood, and I long to show my child just how good life can be. Linda and I together are looking forward to all that lies ahead.

In His love,

Brett

Dear Birth Mother,

Although our circumstances have been different, in many ways you and I have probably shared many of the same emotions. I have certainly experienced shattered dreams, feelings of hopelessness, self pity, despair, and anger at God and others over my inability to change circumstances. I can only imagine that you may have experienced many of these same emotions.

I had always assumed that at some point in my life I would have a child and experience motherhood. Although I was older when I married, my dreams of having a child and being a full-time homemaker were still very much intact. My husband Brett is a wonderful man, totally devoted to me, and shared my dream of wanting children. I had no doubt that he would be a loving, engaged father.

As the years passed, our dreams of children always seemed beyond our reach. Much of my frustration came from realizing I had no control over the situation. Nothing I did, including taking fertility drugs, could change the reality of what the doctors called "unexplained infertility." No problem could be identified, no solution could be found.

Slowly, I realized that God was asking me to relinquish my dream of having my own baby. Slowly, as I embraced the full disappointment and the sense of loss, I began to realize that God must have another plan for Brett and me. As Brett and I began praying about adoption, it became clear that the door of adoption was beginning to open, and open very widely. As painful as this has been, I have learned that if we are willing to give up our dreams and expectations, God has the opportunity to replace those dreams with His dreams for us. And His dreams are always better.

I have now come to embrace adoption wholeheartedly. I am reminded of Jeremiah 29:11 which says, "'For I know the plans that I have for you,' declares the Lord, 'plans for welfare and not for calamity to give you a future and a hope.'"

This verse is a promise for you as well. We know that you have endured some very difficult circumstances. But He does have a future and a hope for you. And you have honored Him by choosing to honor the life within you. Brett and I admire you so for the courage you have shown in carrying and placing your baby for adoption. In today's society when abortion is promoted as an easy solution to an unplanned pregnancy, you have chosen a less traveled path that has required much strength and sacrifice.

We recognize the incredible gift of life that you are giving and we want to support you in any way that we can in your decision. We are certainly comfortable with keeping the lines of communication open in the years ahead and giving you every assurance that your decision to place your baby with us was a good one.

Although we are now strangers, we know our lives will forever be linked by a special little one who has a full, rich life yet ahead.

With deepest affection,

Linda

Chapter Ten

An Act of Terrorism

"Thou wilt keep the nation of steadfast purpose in perfect peace,
because it trusts in Thee. Trust in the LORD forever,
for in GOD the LORD, we have an everlasting Rock."
~Isaiah 26:3-4~

Morning dawned on September 11, 2001. Men and women, carrying a briefcase in one hand and coffee in the other, left their homes for work. Mothers, still in robes, who had been up all night with their new babies, stumbled to the kitchen to scramble eggs and pour juice. Children boarded buses to begin the school day, while a chorus of neighborhood dogs barked a morning greeting. Spouses, conducting business out of town, kissed their mates goodbye at the airport. It was a typical day in America... until 8:45 a.m. when terror ripped across our blue skies and spewed its venom on innocent victims.

Our family had just finished morning devotions. My daughter, Stephanie, and I were in the throes of conquering Algebra One problems. Since we home-school, I generally allow our answering machine to record any messages received during our school hours.

Around 9:30 a.m., I walked into our bedroom to retrieve a book I needed and noticed the light flashing on our answering machine. I normally wait to listen to messages, but today I felt compelled to go over and switch it on. My husband Chuck was on the other end.

"You might want to turn on the television," he said calmly. "The World Trade Center and the Pentagon have just been struck by hijacked American planes." He said more, but that was all I heard as I stood by the phone in disbelief, sorting through my mind how and when to tell Stephanie. I decided to wait until after lunch when most of our studies would be done for the day. In the meantime, a friend called and voiced concern for some of her family members who were on their way to Baltimore to board a plane. She had been watching the news and filled me in on more details of the attack. We prayed for each other and our hurting nation over the phone.

After lunch I shared the news with Stephanie, not knowing how she would react.

"You mean planes crashed into the twin towers?" she asked. "On purpose?"

"Yes, on purpose," I numbly replied. Grief's early cushioning effect, shock, had set in and I was simply going through the motions of explaining events.

Stephanie and I reminisced about our trip to New York City when she was three. She had seen pictures of the Statue of Liberty and wanted so much to climb up to her crown and look out over New York Harbor. As awed as she was by the giant lady holding up her torch beside the golden shore for all the storm-tossed, war-torn, and weary, she was even more impressed with the World Trade Center. She called the buildings "her towers." In a sense she was right. A symbol of American financial strength, they belonged to all of us.

Stephanie had returned home from that memorable trip and built Lego towers, play-doh towers, and cardboard towers. At age

An Act of Terrorism

three, this was one of her earliest impressions of our beautiful, majestic, and powerful country.

On this fateful day, she affirmed ownership and simply responded, "Those were my towers," as if some neighborhood kid had just knocked over her Legos or stepped on her cardboard structures.

We watched the news the rest of the day and off and on throughout the week, trying to make sense out of a senseless tragedy. Stephanie had been quite interested in the newly released movie, *Pearl Harbor*, so this new attack opened up many questions about our history and God's dealings with America since its inception. We mourned as we watched people waving white flags out of the windows of the Trade Center, hoping for a rescue. We cringed at desperate people jumping to their death. We felt compassion for family members who stood by helplessly watching, many in front of a television screen, unable to help their loved ones survive a doomed building. We saw brave firefighters and rescuers, with blatant disregard for their own safety, relentlessly sift through the remaining rubble, propelled by the hope that they might find a survivor. We watched clergymen and volunteers offer a cup of cool water in Jesus' name. We saw people from all religions and walks of life mobilize for relief. We saw our peace-loving President, reminiscent of Lincoln, stand strong and resolute in the face of overwhelming national grief as an example to the American people. We were challenged and encouraged during the memorial service at the National Cathedral in Washington, D.C. President Bush's determination to serve as a strong leader and stand behind the freedom upon which our nation was founded was reflected in his words, "The commitment of our fathers is the calling of our times." His tears revealed his compassion and heart for America. We heard him reassure us with Paul's words from Romans 8:38-39: "For I am convinced that neither death, nor life, nor angels, nor principalities, nor things present, nor things to come, nor powers, nor height, nor depth, nor any other created thing, will be able to separate us from the love of God, which is in Christ Jesus our Lord." We saw Americans on their knees praying. We saw Jesus walking the streets of New York City and offering assistance at the Pentagon. We saw national pride rekindled, as American flags adorned diesel trucks and waved proudly from front doors. We saw a country pulling together and finding strength in adversity. And we felt moved by a nation grieving a joint tragedy.

Collective Grief

The tragic act of terrorism on American soil, ushered in a collective grief affecting our entire nation. We were humbled before God as we watched icons representing America's financial power and military might destroyed. We mourned privately, but we also mourned collectively as a people who share a common heritage and enjoy the benefits of freedom. The loss of life numbered into the thousands, tearing families apart, and leaving homes without spouses, children, and grandparents. We also lost a sense of security, as we were faced with our vulnerability as a nation before our enemies.

We now worry more about the *"what ifs"* of the future with the potential threat to freedom from increased terrorist activity in new forms, such as biological and chemical warfare. Concern for our sons and daughters who may be called upon to enlist for active military duty runs high. I talked to a mom only days ago who was concerned that her nine-year-old son might be eventually drafted into the service. "This conflict could last for many years," she shared, trying to remain calm.

Thankfully, for many, as well as this dear lady, fear has driven them to seek God. Many are open to His love and comfort who were closed to Him previously. They have drawn strength and stability from Scriptures such as Psalm 56:3, "When I am afraid, I will put my trust in You," and Jesus' words in Hebrews 13:5-6,8, "I will never desert you, nor will I ever forsake you, so that we confidently say, 'The Lord is my helper, I will not be afraid, What will man do to me?'... Jesus Christ is the same yesterday and today *(yes)* and forever." They understand that "the name of the Lord is a strong tower; the righteous runs into it and is safe" (Prov. 18:10). They are aware that "righteousness exalts a nation, but sin is a disgrace to any people" (Prov. 14:34) and are turning to God in repentance, so that our great nation might continue to enjoy His blessings.

In talking with people over the days and weeks that followed the attack, I observed individuals working through the grieving process. Some were still in shock; many had moved to anger (at the terrorists, at God, at themselves); some freely cried; others remained stoic, reserved. Those who were able to talk through their thoughts and feelings, however intense, seemed to be faring better than those who kept their feelings bottled up.

Memorial services all over the country offered mourners opportunity to collectively grieve and identify with other hurting people, while receiving comfort from God's Word and prayer. I noticed a resolve to survive this tragedy and come out on the other side a stronger, better people. I also noticed a united spirit in keeping with our name—"The United States of America." When called upon, we, as a people, rise to the occasion. We understand that to overcome evil forces who seek to disrupt freedom, we must stand as a mighty army with God as our captain. God is the author of freedom, and to defend her is to walk according to God's purposes. It is heartening to hear our leaders reaffirm that calling and to show dependence on God, living up to our country's motto which says, "In God We Trust." The Scripture is clear: "Blessed is the nation whose God is the Lord" (Ps. 33:12). He will defend her in time of trouble. God has promised to bless those who bless the seed of Abraham, God's chosen people Israel (Gen. 12:3). Even in the face of persecution, our country remains resolute in defending the land of Israel.

In our loss, we must raise our banner higher and band together with God's strength and might to bring good out of chaos. The question now is, how will we make the most of the time and resources God has given us to advance the cause of freedom and godliness?

Redeeming the Time

We write a weekly email newsletter, encouraging growth as we journey through the seasons of life. Below is an article we wrote the day after the assault on America. We include it here to encourage you to channel your grief over our nation's tragedy into service and witness to others:

> Another lovely pre-fall morning. Proof that beauty goes on in the face of ugliness. Like the war prisoner confined to a cell who chose to focus on the small patch of blue sky outside his tiny window, I search for the blue. That isn't difficult, for today blue explodes across the vast expanse of sky, only interrupted by another pleasure—an occasional white puff. I wonder who is searching for the blue patch in New York City and Washington, D.C. today?
>
> I drive down Main Street to run some errands. Life goes on as usual, only faces are more drawn, haggard. Inside the health food store, the little German lady with the clear blue eyes warmly greets me. I had never noticed until today just how blue her eyes are.
>
> "Oh, I'm so glad to see a familiar face this morning," she sighs with relief written on her face, "especially in light of yesterday's events."
>
> "Yes," I reply. "We must keep those precious people in our prayers."
>
> She nods, affirming my comment while ringing up my goods. I search for more opportunities to seize a

An Act of Terrorism

moment of witness. I had shared my faith with her in the past and she seemed to understand. As I am ready to leave, she hands me my bag and looks straight into my eyes, "Take care and have a good day." I return her gaze, our eyes locking for a few seconds. "Yes, and you do the same," I say with a generous smile. A witness given, a warmth exchanged, to ease the rude cold intrusion of yesterday's events on an otherwise gorgeous day....

Black billowy clouds of smoke interrupted the blue sky in New York City and brought despair to thousands. The horrific assault on the United States Tuesday morning September 11 brought America to a shocking standstill and then to her knees as America's churches opened their doors to receive the anxious, angry, confused, and bewildered. A nation that has tried so hard to exclude God welcomes Him in a crisis. It has always been so. God reminded us on Tuesday that our strength is not in economic power or military might but in the name of the Lord our God.

Tragedies have a way of bringing life into perspective. Concerns that were earthshaking on Monday became trivial on Tuesday. Loved ones became more precious, the Lord more dear.

As a believer in the Lord Jesus Christ, I am relieved and thankful to know that the sovereign God of the universe has not abandoned His throne—He is still in control. He reigns supreme! The God who holds the heart of kings in the palm of His hand directs their way (see Dan. 5:21; Prov. 21:1; Ezra 6:22). In His permissive will, He allows evil to advance in order that He might accomplish a greater good than would have otherwise occurred (Gen. 50:20).

As a child of the King of Kings, I understand that my times are in His hand (Ps. 31:15). He is the keeper of my soul (Ps. 121). In Him, I move and breathe and have my very existence (Col. 1:16-17).

With such knowledge of a certain God in uncertain times, I cry with David: "Teach us to number our days, that we may present to You a heart of wisdom" (Ps. 90:12).

The days are evil and our time is short. Yesterday proved that again. Hurting, despairing people are searching for peace and hope. We who know Jesus hold the key that can unlock their misery and set them free. We know that Tuesday's event was just a point in time on God's great eternal continuum. We understand that to know God is to discover meaning in life and death.

What are you doing to redeem the time? In the face of such tragedy, people may be ready to listen to the Savior's message of love, hope, and forgiveness. Be sensitive to that neighbor, store clerk, friend at the gym, or gas attendant. What questions are they asking? Listen to discern spiritual hunger. What word of hope can you offer as a child of God?

Pray with people who call you on the phone and want to talk about the tragedy. Take them to the place of peace—the very throne room of God. Encourage them to find solace in the Scriptures. Philippians 4:4-9 is an excellent passage when dealing with fear and anxiety. I use it often in my counseling practice.

> *Rejoice in the Lord always; again I will say rejoice! Let your gentle spirit be known to all men. The Lord is near. Be anxious for nothing, but in everything by prayer and supplication with thanksgiving let your*

An Act of Terrorism

> *requests be made known to God. And the peace of God, which surpasses all comprehension, will guard your hearts and your minds in Christ Jesus. Finally, brethren, whatever is true, whatever is honorable, whatever is right, whatever is pure, whatever is lovely, whatever is of good repute, if there is any excellence and if anything worthy of praise, let your mind dwell on these things.*

Indeed, a cheerful, joyful spirit can ward off discouragement which is Satan's number one tactic to defeat us. Encourage people to dwell on God's blessings and to look for the lovely, good, and right in life.

Turn your grief into positive action by contributing to the financial needs of the victims' families. The Red Cross is in need of blood. Donate. This is a national grief that will last for many years. Be ready to offer comfort and assistance.

And, finally, fill your mind with the Scriptures (Psalms is an excellent place to start) so that you can be ready when called upon to give a reason for the hope within you!

Life goes on. What will you do with the gift? Are you looking for the blue? Are you making the most of your time? Will you touch a hurting soul with the gospel message today? Will you offer a cup of cool water in Jesus' name?

Part IV

When Death Comes Knocking

*Precious in the sight of the Lord
is the death of His godly ones.*

~Psalm 116:15~

Chapter Eleven

Losing Someone You Love

Earth has no sorrow that Heaven cannot heal.
~THOMAS MORE~

Kayla is dead, Lord. I know that comes as no surprise to You. You simply reached down, whispered her name, and she was gone.

Kayla and I were so different. She seemed cool and confident. I felt shy and awkward. The boys buzzed around Kayla like bees after nectar. The boys confided in me *about* Kayla, as good buddies do. But, somehow, even in my jealousy of Kayla, I felt an admiration and respect for her. In many ways, I wanted to be like Kayla.

Kayla and I grew up in different towns in Tennessee, both small, within an hour of each other. Our fathers served as full-time missionaries with a Christian camping ministry. From babyhood, Kayla and I spent countless summers at camp involved in one way or another in the ministry—sometimes just making pests of ourselves, running in and out of the camp kitchen, snatching food from the large walk-in refrigerator. As we matured, we actually got to help. We peeled an endless heap of potatoes and washed stacks of dishes over a steaming sink, all the while laughing and carrying on as if we were having the time of our lives. We were.

Kayla left for college a year before me. She chose a school we had visited with our camp youth group during a "College for a Weekend" trip. I enrolled the next fall.

By the time I arrived on campus, Kayla was an old pro at doing this college thing. Again, she appeared to glide around with an air of confidence. My confidence level had not improved all that much. One thing I did know—Kayla and I both wanted to love and serve the Lord, and we were in this place to learn how to do it right.

In October of that year, Kayla chose to help at another Christian camp for a weekend retreat. The camp owned horses. Kayla adored horses. Not many things were more special to Kayla than camping and horseback riding, except maybe boys. Kayla was riding bareback with a young camper when something spooked their horse. The horse reared up and Kayla, sitting behind the little girl, slid off to the ground, knocking her head on a rock. Kayla was immediately rushed to the hospital where she underwent surgery. Her folks flew in from Tennessee to be with her. Back at school, we were all fervently praying for Kayla's recovery, but Kayla never woke up.

Kayla never woke up, Lord. I remember the shock we all felt when news reached campus. There were so many different reactions. Some quietly walked away. Others verbally lamented. One fellow tried to right everything by saying how happy Kayla was in heaven, that we should not be grieved by her absence, but excited for her homegoing. Most of us looked at him in disgust. It was just too soon to hear those words. We needed to grieve for awhile.

I was one of those mourners who chose to run. I pushed open the heavy cafeteria doors and bolted out, hot tears running down my cheeks. I ran down the hill to the porch of the administration building. I had sat there many a time reflecting on life. Now I sat reflecting on death. All the *"hows"* and *"whys"* and *"what fors"* came charging into my mind like unwelcome guests.

Later, at the graveside service in Tennessee, my dad grabbed me and squeezed me like I'd never known before. I'll never forget that crushing embrace, as daddy wept with uncontrollable sobs. I knew he was not only thinking of Kayla and her family, but also about me. I could have been the one in that grave. At that moment, the thought seemed more than daddy could bear—he had lost his firstborn son several years earlier.

Back on campus, Lord. Same dorm, same classes, same friends—except for Kayla. The sameness, permeated with sadness, is so loud. Doesn't anyone realize things aren't the same? That they never will be? I want to run away and hide from the noisy sameness. I cover my ears and run to you, Lord. Where else can I go? You are my Refuge, my Strength, my Comfort. I can't bring Kayla back, but someday I will see her again. We'll be with You forever, talking and laughing just like old times, only much better.

Thanks for whispering my name, Lord, and enabling me to hear You above the deafening pain. Thanks for showing me I don't have to have all the answers. I just need to trust the One who does.

Reflections on Death

We have made many trips to the cemetery since that time twenty-eight years ago. Each time I encounter death up front and personal, either in our family or with close friends, I experience a barrage of thoughts and feelings. Death causes me to reflect, to do some healthy soul-searching, and to depend on my God for grace and strength, when I feel as though the ground has caved in under my feet.

When we decided to write a book on grieving, I pulled out my concordance and traced all the words having to do with grief throughout Scripture. Time after time, I met hope on the pages of God's Word, not despair, but hope—even exhilaration at the prospect of saying goodbye to this life and hello to the next. As I reflected on God's truths, I discovered some realities about death.

First of all, **death is certain.** Everyone living today will some day die. Psalm 89:48 says, "What man can live and not see death? Can he deliver his soul from the power [hand] of Sheol?" I have no control over death. It is certain; it is a fact of life. I can fight it, but it will eventually win.

Secondly, **death is no respecter of persons.** The young die as well as the old. The unprepared die as well as the prepared. The wise and foolish both die. Psalm 49:10-12 says that,

> *...even wise men die; the stupid and the senseless alike perish and leave their wealth to others. Their inner thought is that their houses are forever and their dwelling places to all generations; they have called their lands after their own names. But man in his pomp will not endure; he is like the beasts that perish.*

Thirdly, **we take nothing with us to the grave.** Psalm 49:16-17 says, "Do not be afraid when a man becomes rich, when the glory of his house is increased; for when he dies he will carry nothing away; his glory will not descend after him."

Fourthly, **death is a result of sin.** In Genesis 2:16-17, God says to Adam, "From any tree of the garden you may eat freely; but from the tree of the knowledge of good and evil you shall not eat, for in the day that you eat from it you shall surely die." Adam and Eve's disobedience to God's direct command ushered in physical death as well as spiritual death or separation from God in hell. But God's plan was for us to live with Him forever, so He sent His only begotten Son to earth to pay sin's price to buy us back to Himself.

Fifth, **God offers eternal life after death to those who receive His Son.** When Jesus suffered willingly in our place on the cross, He satisfied God's righteous demands for sin's payment. He tasted death for us, and forever removed the sting. He defeated death by His work on the cross, taking our punishment upon Himself, in order that we might live forever. 1 Corinthians 15:54 and 57 teaches this truth, "'Death is swallowed up in victory. O Death, where is your victory? O Death, where is your sting?'… thanks be to God, who gives us the victory through our Lord Jesus Christ." Though our physical bodies eventually die and decay, our inner man grows brighter and more alive the closer we get to eternity (2 Cor. 4:16).

Jesus secured the cure for sin and made heaven a reality for those who would accept His gift. Even if I had been the only person on the earth, Jesus still would have submitted to the agony of the cross, in order that the blood cleansing wash of His death might provide forgiveness for all my sin, as well as promise me a future in heaven with Him when my physical body dies.

John 3:16 emphasizes the hope we have in Jesus, "For God so loved the world [place your name here], that He gave His only begotten Son, that whoever believes in Him shall not perish, but have eternal life." God has planted within every human heart a restless longing for eternal life, for God Himself.

John Maxwell once said, "For the Christian, death does not end with a period or a question mark. It ends with a comma; life continues on with God."

Sixth, **God views the death of His godly ones as precious,** for they are finally at home with Him, able to enjoy all the delights that He has been preparing for them all their lives. We are each dying even as we live. Life is a mere shadow of the reality to come. The entire process is a long road eventually leading home. Entrance into heaven is truly the believer's crowning moment! If you fear that your loved one did not know the Lord Jesus Christ, hold on to the hope that perhaps in his final moments he did indeed make peace with God.

And finally, **death makes us hungry to know certain things.** Death puts life into perspective. David's prayer in the Psalms reveals his understanding of the brevity of life and certainty of death: "So teach us to number our days, that we may present to You a heart of wisdom"(Psalm 90:12).

We may ponder: *What have I contributed to those around me? What legacy will I leave when I die? What should I be doing now to make a difference for Christ in the world around me? Will I be ready to meet God when I die?* Such thoughts are good and help each one of us discover purpose and meaning in life and death as we progress in our healing journey.

Dealing With Death

One of our favorite Bible stories is found in John 11. Lazarus, Jesus' close friend, is sick and his grieving sisters send for Jesus. By the time He arrives, Lazarus has been dead for four days. A close look at the account reveals varying grief reactions among the primary characters: Mary, Martha, and Jesus.

Martha, organized and in charge, takes the initiative to meet Jesus as He arrives in Bethany. Confronting Jesus, seemingly perturbed that He is late, she says, "Lord, if You had been here, my brother would not have died. Even now I know that whatever You ask of God, God will give You" (John 11:21-22). In her deep grief, Martha falls prey to the "if only" game and appears stuck in the past, but then she expresses hope in Christ's ability to connect with God at this moment. Martha had not lost her faith in Jesus in the midst of her grief.

Jesus doesn't beat around the bush; He gets straight to the point by telling Martha that her brother will rise again. She responds with a general assertion that her brother will rise again in the future resurrection, but Jesus means that He will raise Lazarus today!

This story confirms that God does not always operate on our timetable. According to His divine purpose, He knows the exact moment to intervene. When God comes to us in our grief, He will always reaffirm His promises. Jesus says to Martha, "I am the resurrection and the life; he who believes in Me will live even if he dies, and everyone who lives and believes in Me will never die. Do you believe this" (John 11:25-26)?

When we recognize Jesus and listen to Him, He confronts us with His truth and comfort. Martha confesses faith, but still doesn't fully comprehend what Jesus is trying to tell her. I wonder what Martha's feelings were at this poignant moment of revelation? Relief? Comfort? Overwhelming emotion? Her response in verse 27 almost seems flat in light of what Jesus has just told her about Himself. Martha said to Him, "Yes, Lord; I have believed that You are the Christ, the Son of God, even He who comes into the world." She answers Jesus as if spewing off a catechism. She can't absorb that the God of the universe is standing before her ready to meet her need right then. I don't think Martha can withstand the intensity of the revelation or process it fully. I wonder what Jesus would have said next if Martha had stuck around, rather than leaving, after her response to Jesus. Sometimes, we too run from Jesus when the truth gets too intense. We need to stay and allow Him to speak more to us.

On this side of Jesus' resurrection, John 11:25-27 appears to me like one of those "Touched by an Angel" moments when Monika lights up and reveals God's truth to a needy soul, who tears up and falls to his knees in worship before God. Not so here. Martha affirms belief in Jesus as the Son of God, but misses the compelling truth that He is the resurrection and the life! As with Martha, death forces us to examine our belief system. What are we hanging onto for strength? Where do we turn for comfort? What do we really believe about God? Sometimes we limit God's miracles by where we are in our spiritual journey.

Martha then retrieves Mary who is mourning in the house. Those who have truly encountered Jesus in their grief will direct others to Him. From earlier encounters, Mary— quiet, relational, and reflective—had enjoyed a rich relationship at Jesus' feet. Martha was always serving Jesus, frustrated that Mary was not helping her prepare food. Perhaps, in this instance, God ordered things in such a way so that Martha could finally experience a personal one-on-one encounter with the Lord. In her desperation, Martha was finally pushed beyond her busyness to seek out a quiet moment with Jesus. Grief intrudes on our lives to such an extent, that we are forced to lay aside all other distractions for a time and concentrate on the Lord.

Mary rises quickly when she learns that Jesus is here. Mary's immediate response upon seeing Jesus is the same as any other encounter she'd had with her Lord—she "fell at His feet" (John 11:32). She weeps freely (vs. 33). Mary was used to being at Jesus' feet. For her, it was as natural as breathing to want to be close to Jesus. Grief had not altered her desire, but only intensified it. As with Mary, our habitual times with the Lord in the quietness of His presence will carry us through times of grief. Mary expresses the same concern that Martha did: "Lord, if You had been here, my brother would not have died" (John 11:32). She, too, expresses faith, but limited perspective.

Likewise, we who love the Lord and believe in His abilities, sometimes wonder where He was when our loved one was sick. Limited by our own finite reasoning, we wonder why He did not heal the person. Grief drove both Martha and Mary to the Lord. They each had differing emotional responses, but arrived at the same conclusion about Jesus, namely that He was able to heal their brother. Jesus allowed Martha and Mary to grieve in their own way. One way was not necessarily more spiritual than another. Sometimes, those who seem the closest to God are asking the same why questions as those who are not as close.

When Jesus saw Mary's tears, He wept. The God of the universe, Creator of mankind, originator of life, lover of man is moved by her pain. He literally groaned at the ill effects of sin upon mankind. He was angry at the root cause of sorrow—SIN. Angry that sin had so crippled, debilitated, hindered, and upset the peace and well-being of His perfect creation—man. As the God-man, Jesus identifies with us in our grief because He, too, was human; He knows what it is to feel emotional pain. Even though He knew He would raise Lazarus as a testimony to the glory of His future resurrection, He wept. We must not fear the tears nor hold them back. We know the victorious outcome, but our human condition requires tears of healing.

In His grief, Jesus goes to work and pulls Martha into His plan. He channels her grief into action. Jesus says, "Remove the stone," but Martha argues, "Lord, by this time there will be a stench, for he has been dead four days" (John 11:39). Martha is still consumed by a corpse instead of dwelling on Jesus. She is still limited by death's constraints, but Jesus isn't! She thinks she knows more than Jesus, so has to offer Him a word of caution. Sometimes, when God is ready to perform a miracle in our lives, we resist. We argue and make excuses. Why? Because our spiritual vision is limited. We don't fully trust in God's power to perform according to His promises.

Jesus goes on to remind Martha of their earlier conversation. "Did I not say to you that if you believe, you will see the glory of God?" (John 11:40). Jesus prays first, thanking God for what He is about to do, even before seeing any tangible results. He prays first, then acts. He hungers for this experience to draw the Jews surrounding the tomb to God. Do we look for ways to thank God even in the midst of our grief? He is with us in the midst of our deepest agony. Thank Him for His presence. Thank Him for the life of the deceased, for the time you had together, for the impact of his life and death on those around him. Let your thankfulness draw others to Christ.

After Jesus thanks God, He cries out with a loud voice, "Lazarus, come forth" (John 11:43). As Master over death, Jesus has to say "Lazarus" or everyone who had died would have come forth. He does not choose to raise everyone. He is selective. Jesus, the very source of life, speaks the word of life. Through His triumphant shout, Jesus proclaims victory over death. All creation knows that death can not stand in the face of Jesus. It must recoil and slink back into the shadows. To encounter Jesus is to encounter life! "The man who had died came forth, bound hand and foot with wrappings, and his face was wrapped around with a cloth. Jesus said to them, 'Unbind him, and let him go'" (John 11:44). Lazarus, bound by death's stronghold, is delivered by Jesus' mighty power. Freedom! Jesus embodies life. Lazarus has a personal encounter with the living Christ who sets him free from death's shackles.

Clearly, from this biblical account, we can see that Jesus comes to us as we deal with the death of a loved one. He accepts our varied emotions and weeps with us. When we deal with death from Jesus' perspective, we understand that death is only temporary. We will be with our believing loved ones again, for He has said, "I am the resurrection and the life; he who believes in Me will live even if he dies" (John 11:25).

Part of the healing as you deal with the death of a loved one comes from celebrating the life of the deceased. Some view the funeral or memorial service as an open and shut book on the person's life. Supporters gather to grieve the passing, by remembering the person and his contribution to the world around him. They walk out of the cemetery and resume life as usual, many times with little or no mention of the deceased again. However, for the family and close friends, the funeral is merely a starting place for the healing that cherished memories can provide.

Celebrating the Life, Sharing the Memories

As you work through your own time of intense grief, reflect on the special moments you shared with the deceased. Remember a special outing, hobby, or holiday that you enjoyed together. Think about the laughter you shared. Maybe you enjoyed an annual fall hike in the mountains, or you baked cookies together every Christmas and distributed them to the neighbors. You may be possessive of these memories at first, but as you heal and are ready, allow someone else to be a part of that special event that you cherished with your loved one. The love you shared with that person can be celebrated by doing that favorite activity with another person. This may be difficult in the early stages of grief, but as you mend, it can prove quite beneficial and fulfilling. It may be the first time since the death that you feel alive again.

Write down how your loved one's life touched you. Consider the following questions: How am I a better person today because of him? You might look up Galatians 5:22-23 and identify the fruits of the Spirit that showed forth in your loved one's life. Ask yourself, "How can I now demonstrate some of these fruits in celebration of his memory?"

Some have been helped by making a memory book with photos illustrating cherished activities shared together. This may be especially beneficial in helping a child deal with the loss of a loved one. A grieving child may want to draw a picture of his deceased sibling playing dolls, or of his father riding bikes with him. As a therapist, this activity is especially helpful, as I learn what the child is thinking about the person who died. The drawing is a beginning place—it opens the child up to explore what he is thinking and feeling today. Art therapy uses some of the past to get the child in the present. I once counseled a six-year-old who was still wearing his dad's jacket to bed four weeks after his father's death. The mother came to me concerned that the child's behavior was excessive. I explained to her that the boy was still in the early stages of grief, and that the jacket was a tangible item that kept father and son connected, much the same way a baby clings to a pacifier or blanket for comfort.

While memorializing the deceased can be therapeutic, it can also be overdone. I dealt with one man who enshrined his wife with pictures and candles in his den. He literally turned his deceased wife into an idol. Someone once observed, "I've only known two perfect people in my life, and never personally met either one face-to-face—Jesus and my wife's deceased husband!" The mourner can overplay his loved one's good points and forget the bad. For true healing to occur, the grieved needs to recognize that there were some bad aspects to the relationship as well as good ones. Tell yourself the truth about the relationship.

You may be angry because death closed the door on any future work on the relationship. Write out *all* your feelings as they come. A daily two-minute exercise is helpful. Start out with the phrase, TODAY I FEEL _____. Express your anger, sadness, loneliness, fear, curiosity, pain, shock, guilt, confusion, and any other emotions you may be feeling. Try to identify the emotional triggers. Don't be afraid to address God with your feelings. He understands and wants to help.

Keep a journal of God's faithful dealings with you as you travel through your grief journey; for example, how God worked in the life of a relative at the funeral service, or how He provided an indescribable peace for you at the graveside. Although you may not feel like reading the Bible or praying, some of the best comfort you can find is in the Psalms. Read until God gives you a special verse or passage all your own. Write it on a three by five card, post it in a handy place, and read it often throughout the day. Soon you will find yourself quoting the verses during sleepless nights. There is no way to underestimate the healing power of the Scriptures in dealing with grief. There is no substitute for God's Word. It is designed to bring comfort.

The soothing touch of music is another powerful healing tool. Sometimes, it can reach places in the heart that nothing else quite can. After the sudden death of my college friend Kayla, I called a friend in another dorm. My friend had a rich baritone voice and was known for singing a particular hymn. That night I asked him to sing it to me over the phone. Whenever I hear that song, I think of the comfort Dan brought me that night many years ago by a simple act of kindness. Many others have been blessed in a similar way through music.

Continue to talk about your loved one freely. Society generally allows the mourner two to three days to grieve. After the funeral, everyone goes home. Everyone is supposed to be okay, when in reality the funeral is only the beginning of the healing process. The grieving one has to go back home and pick up life without the other person, many times without the needed support of other caring individuals. The mourner may feel like a car with a missing spark plug. The car can run, but it's not a very smooth ride. The grieving one may find help in a support group or the listening ear of another family member or friend. Find someone who feels comfortable talking about the deceased. You need this emotional outlet, so that you don't have to pack up all your cherished memories and move within yourself. Keep talking as the need to do so arises.

You may find it healing to write a letter to the deceased. Express thanks for all the things that made your relationship special. Below is a sample letter written to a deceased husband. Simply share in your letter what is on your heart.

Dear _____,

I miss you so desperately. The pain is overwhelming at times.

Last night I dreamed about you all night long only to awaken and find you weren't beside me.

I was so sad and alone. I was frustrated that you were no longer there to share an intimate moment. I haven't had to harness sexual feelings for a long, long time. I guess it's good I can even feel. For a long time, I was simply numb.

Tonight, I thought I heard you pull in the driveway. My heart skipped a beat. But it was just a neighbor coming home from work. I still forget sometimes that I don't need to throw an extra potato in the oven for your lunch the next day.

I miss your warm, inviting eyes, the way you use to hold me close and look down at me with those smiley eyes.

I miss the times we would snuggle up on our sides in bed together, our legs crooked in exactly the same place—a perfect fit. One of us would say something outstandingly witty or ridiculously funny, and we would get so tickled. I miss that good belly laugh in the dark at the close of day.

I miss praying together at the breakfast table in the mornings.

I even miss our petty arguments.

I miss our long talks in the car on Friday nights. Our walks on the beach in summer. The way you always seemed to handle a problem, making things I made difficult look so simple. The way you loved our children.

I miss my best friend.

Tonight, I think I realized for the first time—I mean really realized—you are not coming back. The thought struck me head-on like a diesel truck. I felt panicky. I couldn't breathe. Then I remembered when you were alive, how you would calm me when I felt anxious. You would sit with me and talk me through it. I'm listening for your voice, your words. The memory helps.

I know I'll see you again in heaven. Our love will be perfect then—different, but perfect.

I know if you were here, you'd tell me what a fantastic place you are in. I'm jealous. I want to be there with you.

I know God has a reason for taking you and leaving me. Someday, perhaps I'll know. For now, I am just so incredibly sad. People tell me that in time the tears will stop. But I don't think I will ever fully stop grieving until I see you again. Somehow, I believe that's okay. The occasional tears are a healing wash. And someday, God will wipe all tears away, for in that grand and glorious place, there will be no death or sadness, just everlasting joy.

Someone sang your favorite song last Sunday—"Turn Your Eyes Upon Jesus"—and I wept in the pew until I thought my head would explode. I miss you beside me in church with your arm around me. I always looked forward to that special time of closeness after a busy week.

I wish I could wake up from this awful nightmare. I want to run away, but there is nowhere to hide from this penetrating pain.

I don't understand God's plan, but I rest in it. He is my only source of relief. How exciting to realize that you are with Him now. I can hardly believe it! You must be so happy. I suppose I wouldn't want to cheat you out of that much joy. But then, you know me—selfish.

Until we see each other again, I cling to the verse a dear friend shared with me when she lost her husband,

"For your husband is your Maker, whose name is the Lord of hosts" (Isa. 53:5). I know He will care for me.

Love always,

Your devoted wife

Finally, when you are ready, don't feel guilty for moving on with your life. You have permission to do things differently than your loved one would have if you desire to do so. You can form new attachments, and it is indeed healthy to do so. You will never forget your loved one, but at some point in your grieving process, you will be ready to begin life anew. As you progressively turn your pain over to God, in time you will feel whole again.

Helping a Child Cope With Death

The grandchildren had just come into the room to sing her favorite songs. Lined up like stair steps, they offered Mom Rife the sweet gift of children's voices filling the air with innocent peace. The lilting music sliced through death's thick cloud hovering over her bed. For a few moments, all in the room were transported beyond. Dad Rife knelt by Mom's bed and held her hand. "It's okay to go, honey. Let Jesus take you," he softly said, then bowed his head in prayer. Seconds later, Mom lunged forward, her eyes shot open, and then she laid back on the pillow, eyes closed and at peace.

Mom Rife battled cancer and Alzheimer's for about five years. Like a competent general in command of his troops, Dad took charge of her care. He monitored dietary requirements, supervised doctors' appointments, and managed affairs around the clock.

In August 1992, two weeks before her fiftieth wedding anniversary, Mom's condition deteriorated, and she quietly slipped into a coma. Determined to keep her at home during her final days, Dad called in Hospice to supervise her care and monitor the emotional needs of the family.

Eileen and I had planned a trip to visit my folks before the start of a new school year. We did not realize how serious Mom's condition was.

Several other family members were already in the room when we arrived at my house. Walking into the front bedroom, I saw my brothers, sister, and a few nieces and nephews huddled around Mom's bed. I paused in the doorway, mentally and emotionally preparing myself for what lay ahead. I did not want to believe Mom was slipping away from us. The whole scene seemed so unreal, as if I were viewing a movie. I felt detached, yet at the same time anxious to become part of the group surrounding Mom. In a matter of seconds, I was by her side, a thousand questions flooding my mind.

I was glad Dad chose to involve Hospice rather than put Mom in the hospital. The decision was a wise and comforting one, especially as each of the adult family members took turns caring for Mom. Being actively involved in her care helped us in the transition process. We felt useful, rather then merely pacing back and forth in a hospital room or lobby, or being shooed away by overly busy doctors and nurses. We could actually DO something for Mom to show our continued love for her, even though our care was merely keeping her as comfortable as possible until the end came. As she could not respond to us, we did not know for sure how much of our care or words she understood. But we drew comfort from being a part of her final days. Our active participation helped ease us through the difficult grieving process that lay ahead.

One of my fondest memories during this difficult time, occurred shortly before Mom passed away. One afternoon, on our back porch, Dad and I embraced each other and sobbed. In the past, Dad and I had connected to one another on an intellectual level, but rarely on an emotional level. The only other time I had ever seen Dad cry was when his father died. In our mutual need, we reached out to one another on an emotional level in a way that I will never forget. Dad needed me and I needed him. Now, when I counsel grieving clients, I often share that moment in my life as a good outcome of my grieving experience.

The day Mom left us, each family member grieved in his own way. Dad had been grieving for the past five years as he watched his wife's health progressively slip away. In a way, her death finalized his lingering episode with grief, while it merely ushered ours in. As I watched him immediately after Mom's passing, I was reminded of David's experience with death in 2 Samuel 12:15-23. His baby boy, born illegitimately by Bathsheba, was gravely ill. While the child lingered, he prayed and fasted. I'm sure he did everything humanly possible to help the baby. As King, he probably called in the most skilled and expensive medical specialists. But once the child died, he rose from prayer, washed his face, worshiped the Lord, and then went on about his business. Those around him questioned such actions in the face of his loss, but he replied, "While the child was still alive, I fasted and wept; for I said, 'Who knows, the Lord may be gracious to me, that the child may live.' But now he has died; why should I fast? Can I bring him back again? I shall go to him, but he will not return to me."

Although healing still needed to occur in Dad's life, Mom's death brought a certain closure to his grief and an assurance that God had chosen to perform His will in this particular way. Dad chose to move forward in response to God's answer.

Most in the family, including us, were miles behind Dad and had only taken a few steps in our healing journey. Having cared for Mom in a comatose state for a week, we had moved past the denial stage. Some, perhaps, were now dealing with anger, others were numb, but moving towards acceptance.

With a house full of people each dealing with Mom's death in a unique way, I stepped back to observe my girls' reactions. This was their first close-up confrontation with death. Our youngest was six, and seemed absorbed in her own world and the activity of her young cousins. Our middle daughter was ten, and had a more realistic outlook on the situation, and a matter-of-fact attitude toward Grandma's death. Both girls, however, remained quiet and chose to play with "the Ohio cousins" throughout our visit. Perhaps they were in shock, the reality of death not fully impacting their world. Maybe, the blessed numbness one feels in the early days of grief had bathed their minds and guarded their hearts until they could find full vent back at home. I don't fully know, but I suspect the cousins talked amongst themselves as children often do.

I remember eight-year-old cousin Benjamin slipping into Mom's room before the coroner arrived. As I observed from the hallway, I noticed Benjamin creeping up to her bedside, leaning his arms on the side of the bed, and peering deeply into Mom's face. He lingered for a few moments as if struggling to understand death, as if somehow, someway Mom's face would unravel a secret answer to the mystery of death. In that tender moment, the scene appeared like a Norman Rockwell painting. How simple and yet how profound in the stillness of that suspended moment. How innocent and yet how wise. Benjamin's face mirrored all our faces, with all our questions and surging emotions.

Our oldest girl, now entering her teen years, stayed close to the adults, quietly listening to us memorialize Mom and organize details for her service, which we desired more than anything to be a tribute to her godly testimony and her fifty years of faithfulness to Dad.

While I grieved Mom's death, I agonized as I watched my children let go of someone they loved. Both Eileen and I assured them that it was okay to cry, to feel the pain, and to talk about Grandma. Remembering Grandma in conversation would "keep her with us."

To allow the girls freedom to grieve, to experience all of life—death being a very real part of it—would help them grow and learn to rely on God more heavily in the face of life's realities.

Dr. Alan D. Wolfelt, a specialist in grief therapy, encourages caring adults to help children through their time of loss. He says, "if adults are open, honest and loving, experiencing the loss of someone loved, can be a chance for children to learn about both the joy and pain that comes from caring deeply for other people."[1] Keeping in mind that each child will grieve in his own way according to his age, personality, and circumstances, below are some suggestions to aid in the process.

1. Be truthful about the events of the death. Sometimes, adults try to protect the child from hurt by pretending nothing happened or by minimizing the events surrounding the death. In reality, the child often knows more than adults give him credit for. He will pick up on the whisperings and the changed routine. A child, already learning about the world, craves the truth. He will appreciate an explanation presented in simple, concrete terms.

2. Assure the child that it is okay to grieve. Acknowledge the child's feelings. Often, a child will move in and out of the grief stages. Accept this behavior as part of the healing process. Serve as a model by expressing your own feelings. Be available to listen and to talk. Don't be afraid to cry in front of the child. Be patient as the child exhibits varying grief reactions, such as crankiness, regressive behavior, anxiety, fear, guilt, denial, hostility, disorganization, and anger. These are all normal responses to the death of a loved one. What he needs now is a loving, supportive adult to walk with him through the process. Try to maintain a stable schedule as much as possible. Don't shut him off from familiar people. He has already lost one close person. Provide him access to friends and other family members who can assure him of continued love and support.

3. Allow freedom for questions. Hedda Sharapan, a colleague of Fred Rogers and grief specialist, writes that one of the best ways an adult can protect a child against fantasy surrounding death "is to provide him with simple and straightforward answers to his questions and ample opportunities to let an adult know what questions he has."[2]

Keep a listening ear attuned to the child. He may need to ask certain questions over and over, so be flexible and patient. Repetition helps the child adjust to the loss. Taking the time and effort to lovingly answer questions shows the child that you respect his thoughts and feelings. Keep in mind that it is not always the exact words that are used, but the atmosphere in which they are communicated. Stay warm, open, and reassuring. A believer in the Lord Jesus Christ has every reason to remain positive and hopeful, even in the face of life's gravest tragedy. Loving communication of truth from God's Word, praying with the child, and verbally affirming your faith in the heavenly Father can point the child to God, the source of all comfort.

4. Observe the child's behavior. Depending on the age and personality of the child, he may not talk about the death, but will often relay his feelings in other ways. A common vent is through play. Notice how the child interacts with dolls, puppets, or building blocks. He may express anger by repeatedly stacking blocks and then knocking them over. The child may bury her doll in the sand or have a mock funeral. Acting out can provide a healthy vent to the child's emotions as he processes his feelings. Art, music, and dreams can also provide expression, and can alert an observant adult as to how the child is internalizing the grief.

5. Include the child in your grief. Resist the temptation to become absorbed in your own grief. Yes, there are times when each griever needs to be alone, but make sure you are providing plenty of opportunity for the child to share the grief with you. Don't push him away. He needs you and you need him. Hold each other often. Talk about the deceased loved one. Share memories together. Avoid the fantasy that the dead person will return, a natural thought in a young child's mind. Depending on the child's age and maturity, allow him to participate in the funeral arrangements. Allow the child to comfort you and thus aid in his healing. Chuck Swindoll once shared this story: "A little girl lost a playmate in death and one day reported to her family that she had gone to comfort the sorrowing mother. 'What did you say?' asked her father. 'Nothing,' she replied, 'I just climbed up on her lap and cried with her.'" Sharing your grief together will provide security for you as well as the child.

Expect holidays to be a challenge, especially the first ones following the death. Sister Teresa McIntier, a registered nurse, suggests that adults help the child develop his own personal healing rituals. Since a child's world revolves around rituals of many kinds, healing rituals can play a natural role in easing the child's transition through the pain of losing. One grieving child suggested that his deceased sister's picture become the Christmas angel at the top of the tree. This act of remembrance started a family tradition. Another hung a stocking in memory of the deceased loved one. In the weeks preceding Christmas day, each family member wrote or drew something in memory of the person and placed it in the stocking. On Christmas day, each member took turns drawing from the stocking, and reading or explaining the gift he had made in memory of the deceased.

6. Be alert to signs indicating outside intervention is needed. While most behaviors are normal following a death, watch for prolonged grieving patterns. If a child threatens suicide, develops panic attacks, or abuses others, get professional help. Also seek help if the child engages in illegal behaviors, such as drug abuse or crime, or if his grades drop, or he demonstrates anti-social behavior.

※

Grieving the death of a loved one is one of the hardest things you will ever do, but it is also one of the greatest opportunities to draw close to the Lord. He stands ready with open arms to meet you and your children in your deepest grief. He is weeping with you. Picture yourself and your family in His loving embrace, receiving strength and comfort from Him.

Part V

When Someone Leaves

Chapter Twelve

When a Child Leaves Home

*Only yesterday she stepped into my heart,
and I will never be the same again.*

The air was crisp for a late August morn—early signs of autumn. I felt an unusual anticipation in the new day. As I walked briskly around the block, I noticed moms and dads with their children leaving front doors and approaching the bus stop. Some children seemed excited by the thought of a fresh school year, running happily ahead of their parent. Most of these ambitious upstarts were "first-timers." Having never darkened the doors of a schoolhouse, they were now eagerly awaiting the new thrill of kindergarten. Older, wiser children, fully aware of what lay before them, lagged wearily behind and were actually pushed forward by their parent.

I was most intrigued by the parents of the kindergartners. Some emitted a great big sigh of relief, I suppose at the thought of finally delivering their young one into the care of another. Others stood motionless with a sleepy blank stare smeared across their faces, seemingly oblivious to the import of the day. A few others stood quietly weeping.

The "weeping" crowd tugged at my heart, especially since my neighbor fell into that category. As I rounded the corner to come back home from my morning walk, I observed Carla standing by the roadside with five-year-old Stephen. With hair slicked back and bus card securely tied around his neck, he came flying into my yard.

"Mrs. Rife, Mrs. Rife, I get to go to school today!" Stephen fairly gleamed as he chattered on about his upcoming day. I gave Stephen a generous squeeze, wished him well in his newfound venture, and sent him back to his mom, still waiting at the roadside.

As I reached to open my front door, Carla yelled over, "I think I'm going to start bawling." I thought for a minute and responded, "That's okay, Carla, I'm a mom too, and that's just what moms do."

The image of Carla standing sadly by the roadside anticipating that first momentous goodbye in her son's life plagued me all day long. As the thought rattled around in my head, the Holy Spirit reminded me that each of us encounter bus stops in our lives. We moms learn early on that motherhood is a lifelong process of letting go. Beginning with the birthing bus stop, we move on to the childhood bus stop, only to move on to the adolescent bus stop, the graduation bus stop, the betrothal bus stop, and I suppose, a life committed to a never-ending line of bus stops, as we observe our grown children make their way in life. We, mentally, once again let go and let God have His way in their lives.

Each bus stop encounter is a fresh taste of grief, a struggle to let go, to relax and allow God to carry that precious cargo to His desired destination. As we watch the bus round the corner and disappear out of sight, we force a goodbye and the tears come. Each stage requires mental and emotional adjustment, especially at graduation time when we can no longer deny the truth that the kids are growing up and out.

Psalm 46:10 says, "Cease striving [let go, be still, relax] and know that I am God." God comes to us in our goodbyes and reminds us that He is in control. We are in His loving care and so are our cherished ones. God may ask us to say goodbye to one bus, but hello to another bus, one filled with all manner of good things just waiting to get off and enter our lives. God delights in filling our lives with His riches. He is faithful to fill the void, first of all with Himself, and secondly with other people and the treasures of life.

Don't fear the bus stops. God designs them for our growth and for His glory. Learn to keep moving on with God. Though your roles may change throughout life, your identity is firmly fixed in Christ. You will always belong to Him and He will always have a unique plan just for you!

Journaling my three girls' growing up years has helped ease my pain. Through tear-stained eyes, I have allowed my writings to be a form of healing, another step in the struggle to loosen the reins and allow my young ponies to dart from their stalls and run free with the wind at their backs. And what a joyous freedom that is for all of us. I feel free because I had the courage to let go. They feel free because mom believed they could soar on the wind, and they are more than ready to do so.

Saying Goodbye Doesn't Mean Forever

Chuck and I stood on our front stoop waving to our oldest daughter as she pulled out of our driveway on her way to Tennessee. With a sly smile, Chuck uttered through clenched teeth, "She doesn't have a clue where she is going." I thought to myself—*Neither do we!* Rachel was concerned about finding her way to a Christian camp. We were concerned about finding our way through the transition years to the empty nest. Rachel did make her ultimate destination. Sometimes, I wondered if Chuck and I would.

As Chuck held the storm door open for me, he joked, "Parenting reminds me of that line in the Jurassic Park movie, 'First comes the oohing and ahhing, and then comes the yelling and the screaming.'" One of the main characters, a scientist, who had previously been to the dinosaur reserve, was explaining the typical reaction of a newcomer to the park. Then, when faced with an actual life-sized dinosaur, reality set in. As new parents, we had experienced our share of "oohs and ahhs." No longer "new kids on the block," we now embraced the glaring reality that parenting is just plain hard work and at times, down right scary. Some days, we just wanted to scream—at our kids, at ourselves for handling a situation badly, or simply to release the pain we felt at saying goodbye to our grown children.

As I said goodbye to Rachel that day on her way to camp, I realized anew that parenting is terminal. It does eventually come to an end, or at least it should under healthy conditions. I spent the year before Rachel's high school graduation, coming to grips with that fact. Grieving her lost childhood and uncertain about my new relationship with her, I snuck behind doors to conceal my tears, scurried off to the bathroom in the middle of dinner to blow my nose, and smothered her with hugs whenever she walked past me.

One day, while washing dishes, I burst into tears. Rachel walked into the kitchen and I immediately opened a cabinet door to hide my face. I didn't want to make her transition from home any harder on her than it already was. I started to leave, but as I turned to walk away, Rachel looked me straight in the eyes, took me in her arms, and squeezed. That "squeeze" opened the door for a closer relationship, as I no longer tried to shut her out of my pain. We could now walk through the transition together. With broken voice, I stammered, "I know you have to leave. That's right and good. Please bear with me as I deal with saying goodbye. Crying is just part of being a mom." Rachel quietly responded, "I know. And guess what? Saying goodbye doesn't mean forever. I'll be back."

Since that time, our second-born, Michelle, has graduated from high school and our last born, Stephanie, prepares to enter high school. Sometimes, I feel as if my head is spinning, as if we live in a house with a revolving door. As changing as our family is right now, I am so thankful for children who love the Lord and want to serve Him with their lives. That reality provides overriding comfort in the midst of flux. Understanding our need for connectedness, our girls have encouraged us through notes, e-mails, and special cards, not to mention warm smiles and hugs.

Last summer, when Rachel spent six weeks teaching English in China, she sent an e-card to her dad with a picture of a galloping white horse on the front. "Dad, I thought you'd like this horse. Thank you for letting me 'run like the wind' and chase the dreams that God has given me—even when they take me to the other side of the world. I love you and I'll see you soon." Later she sent me one. "Mom, I know it's hard for you to have me so far away, but thank you for letting go and letting me fly. Even though you can't hold onto me anymore, there is Someone else Who can, and is. I promise you, I'm safe in His care. I love you, Rachel."

Our second daughter, Michelle, wrote a letter to us on the morning of her high school graduation and placed it on the kitchen table. What an encouragement to our hearts as we read it through teary eyes.

> Mom and Dad,
>
> I don't consider it fair to receive all the praise. The people who really deserve the honor and glory are you. I love you both so much! I know I don't usually tell you that, but I really do. You have done so much for me. Where would I be without you? I am so incredibly blessed to have

been raised by parents who care about my future and most importantly, know Jesus as their personal Savior. Thank you for introducing me to Jesus! Even before I was born, you prayed that I would allow Jesus to have a place in my life. You have been an awesome Christian example to me. I never had to ask if we would be attending church because I knew the answer would be yes.

So, really, it is not all my accomplishment but yours. You made me who I am. You helped me through school and never gave up on me. I thank God for you. I can't imagine where I would be if you had not taken the time to care for me.

Thanks for everything!

Love you both,

Michelle

Our youngest now faces being an "only" child as Michelle enters college this fall. Adjustments face each of us as we guide our last born through the high school years. She continues to encourage us daily with her love for violin, her sweet spirit, and her tender heart toward others, yet we realize that she, too, is pulling away from the nest and growing increasingly independent. How, then, do we lovingly detach from our children as they mature and soar on their own?

Strategies for Loving Detachment

Remember barren Hannah in 1 Samuel chapter one. In fervent prayer she promised to give God her child if He would enable her to conceive. God provided a son and Hannah made good on her promise. When Samuel was weaned, Hannah took him to the temple to live with the priest, Eli. Samuel grew to be a godly judge over all Israel, fulfilling God's divine mission for his life, because his mother was willing to release him to the Lord.

Likewise, Jesus left the comforts of His heavenly home to accomplish a divine mission. Only in the pain of leaving, could good be accomplished. Somehow, I think even His earthly mother Mary understood that He had to be about His Father's business. God enabled her to persist in a lifetime of "letting go" which ultimately led to the most painful release of all—the cross.

The Lord has a divine mission for your child, too. Knowing you have committed him to the Lord will make letting go that much easier when he walks out the front door to build a life of his own. Leaving is the next step in God's fulfillment of His plan for which you prayed!

You grieve as you detach because you are saying goodbye to the past and hello to a brand new day—one that is quite different. Some of the grieving comes as we celebrate the rich memories of our child's past. Every stage of a child's life is one of change; constantly growing; continually surprising us. If a parent loves the child unconditionally, from the beginning he will provide opportunities for the child to mature. At each stage, the parent must assess his child's physical, emotional, spiritual, mental, and social needs, determining how those needs differ from what they were previously. This crucial assessment is all a part of the progressive "letting go" that a parent must do as the child grows.

When our kids were small, I detected a pattern of change about every six months. For two weeks I would wonder why my little girl was extra cranky. Finally, it would dawn on me that she was pushing forward, and I would need to adjust to her growth.

As your child moves through the growth stages, respect what his individual development requires. Two things enable you to do this:

1. Know that God loves your child even more than you do.
2. Put yourself in your child's place. Become a student of your

child. Study his patterns of growth, his interests, his strengths, and weaknesses, and guide him accordingly. This is in keeping with Proverbs 22:6 which says, "Train up a child in the way he should go, even when he is old he will not depart from it."

"In the way he should go" means according to his own natural bent. Admittedly, this discovery about who our children are takes time and, often, trial and error. But if we are diligent observers, we will note some natural tendencies in our children that help us direct them accordingly. As our girls grew, we presented them with varying options for developing their God-given interests and talents. One chose piano, another guitar, still another violin. As they matured, one chose volunteer work, another chose to enter the work force. Life was easier on all of us when we presented four or five options, and let them choose the path to take.

If we force a tree branch to bend in a different direction, eventually it will break. The same principle applies to children. This does not mean that we tolerate sinful behavior, simply that we recognize and respect the child's God-given personality and work with it, rather than against it. Together with God, we gently mold and shape the child into a vessel fit for His service.

Learn to see the world through your child's eyes. Everything is fresh and new to him. The wonder of life compels him to reach out and grab a flower, catch a butterfly, or skip stones in a creek. Spend some time entering his world each day, and rekindle the child within yourself. Search for the teachable moments. I've learned in sixteen years as a home-school mom that my girls often absorbed more in an hour of spontaneous discovery than in a day of forced instruction. Fascination over a starlit evening led to a library trip to check out books about the stars and planets. A turtle who wandered into our yard sparked interest in further research about the little critters.

Be sensitive to your child's "venting moments." These may appear in the form of emotional release, as in frustration or anger.

When a Child Leaves Home

When he is small, he cannot yet articulate his feelings with words, so he acts them out. I remember when Rachel was just a two-year-old. When I took her to bed one evening, she said, "Daddy, I hate you." Rather than become unglued, I saw it as a teachable moment. I simply said, "It's okay if you hate me, because nothing you say or do will ever change the fact that I love you. I will always love you." My statement took the wind out of her sails, and she realized she was still going to have to go to bed.

Look beyond the emotion and listen to what your child is trying to communicate. Thoughtfully direct him to release his feelings in appropriate ways. He may need to be alone for awhile. He may need a chore. At other times, he may need you to hold him and gently pray with him. Sometimes, writing or drawing his feelings can help. Banging them out on a piano can lead to some interesting compositions, if your nerves can withstand the process.

"Venting" may also be precious moments when some of life's toughest questions are asked on the way to soccer practice, while reading a story together at night, or gazing at the stars around a campfire. Make sure you are spending adequate amounts of time with your child to ensure these moments occur. Often, it takes quantity time to get quality time. Some of the best moments are the least expected.

Spend time moving through each stage with your child, so that when the time is right, you can let go. The phases of a child's life will consume differing amounts of energy and time. If you are spending the same amount of time with your twelve-year-old as you did when he was a two-year-old, then you have set up an abnormal dependency. The child becomes an idol when the parent needs the child to stay in a previous stage, hindering him from transitioning to maturity.

A healthy and natural separation occurs around the junior high years, when a young person seeks increased companionship outside the home. He is consumed with learning who he is in relation to others, and where he fits into the world. He may appear distant and moody at times as he processes this phase of his life. This "leaving" can sneak up and surprise a parent if he doesn't know what to expect. Sometimes home-school moms can find this most traumatic, as time spent with the kids is more than the average parent spends. It is critical to adjust mentally, and provide opportunities for healthy detachment. Let them try their wings. Use Proverbs as a study guide to encourage godly friendships. Provide outside classes, volunteer work, missions trips, and church youth groups.

You separate from your teen physically after high school and college, and even more so after marriage, but you do not separate spiritually. Now is the time to pray for your child more than ever. Prayer is the best gift you can offer. Hopefully, you have been praying for him and with him all during his life. The teen may leave, but he cannot escape your prayers. The Father is watching, and your teen is in His arms.

As an increasing number of adult children return home to live, sometimes with grandchildren, the detachment process is blurred. A new set of adjustments are required. Lines must be drawn, expectations discussed, and daily routines mapped out.

The following is a list of things to consider when lovingly detaching from your grown child.

1. Transition times are the hardest. Helping your young person move to complete independence requires thinking through the practical affairs of living. Will your child get a job or go to college? If he chooses college, will he work to pay his way or will you offer financial assistance? Will he purchase a car? When?

Each child and each situation is different, so it is important to sit down together and map out a strategy in keeping with the child's goals and available resources. Savings and checking accounts need to be set up, if they have not been already, and the young person needs to at least understand the basics of balancing a checkbook and maintaining a car.

Carol Kuykendall has written an excellent book published by Focus on the Family entitled, *Give Them Wings*, on preparing for the time your teen leaves home. A church friend loaned the book to me during Rachel's senior year of high school. I found the advice timely, practical, and comforting. I highly recommend it to you for additional help in this time of transition.

2. When your teen is "under his own roof" financially, then he can make his own decisions. As long as you are footing the bill for college or any other venture, your teen is accountable to you and has not fully left. Finance leads to freedom, which leads to independence.

3. Set boundaries before your teen leaves home. Establish some plan for phone calls, e-mails, or letters. If your child has left the home financially independent, then he is no longer a child. He has moved from Ephesians 6:1—"Children, obey your parents in the Lord" to Ephesians 6:2—"Honor your Father and Mother." If he has been taught from the cradle to respect your authority in a way that has been loving and also respectful to him, then most likely, he will continue to honor you through his actions and words. To do so shows true maturity on his part.

Don't overload your grown child with advice. During these transition years, it may seem he needs you one minute and casts you aside the next. Be patient as he moves toward full independence. Allow him to learn what you had to learn by experiencing life. And by all means, keep praying!

4. Give yourself permission to express what you feel. Stuffing emotions may be misconstrued as cold or callous behavior. Letting go of the tears, when needed, made me realize the emotions were not as uncontrollable as I had feared.

I like the segment on the movie, *Father of the Bride,* the night before the wedding. Steve Martin (the dad) is outside their home playing a final game of basketball with his only daughter, Annie. Annie turns to her dad and says, "I've lived here since I was five and I feel like I have to turn in my key tomorrow. You know how you taught me to save everything—my papers, my old retainer, even my magic tricks. I've actually packed up everything in my room. I just didn't want to let it go. I know I can't stay, but I don't want to leave either."

Dad: "That's the thing about life—the surprises. The little things that sneak up and surprise you. It still happens to me."

Annie: "Thanks."

A soft snow begins to fall, and they stop playing to marvel over a snowstorm in California. Silence follows as they stand and look at one another. In that peaceful moment, Annie's father says, "I'll remember this moment the rest of my life."

To the Young Person

In writing this chapter, I asked Chuck what he would say to a young person leaving home for the first time. He jokingly said, "I'd say the same thing I'd say to you when you go to the beauty shop, 'Good luck to ya!'" On a more serious note, here are some things he shared:

❧ **My love and prayers go with you.** We'll be here for you when you need us.

❧ **It's okay to grieve your loss of childhood.** Crying is not a sign of weakness or dependence. Don't try to be strong for "mom."

Share your feelings. Once shared, they don't seem like the monster you thought they were.

🌿 **Remember Whose you are.** God made you and you are accountable to Him. When no one else is watching, God is. If you have received Christ as your Savior and Lord, you have been purchased by the precious blood of Jesus. You belong to Him. "Or do you not know that your body is a temple of the Holy Spirit who is in you, whom you have from God, and that you are not your own? For you have been bought with a price; therefore glorify God in your body" (1 Cor. 6:19-20).

🌿 **Make it a lifetime goal to build an intimate relationship with God.** As you do, He will direct your steps. Michelle and I sat on the beach, soaking up the sun, and watching the waves lap the shore last summer. At one point, she turned to me and said, "Do you ever feel stuck?" I replied, "Yes, there have been times in my life when I have felt that way." Moving into her senior year, she was concerned that she had no clear direction from God for her future beyond high school. I assured her that God would lead one step at a time as she read His Word and talked to Him about every aspect of her life.

Michelle was still uncertain about the next step to take after a year at our local community college, so we asked her to write down what she did know right then. She responded that she learned from a secular college setting that she needed to know how to defend her faith better. She had witnessed to several students and, sometimes, felt stumped by their questions. She had encountered professors with opinions contrary to the Bible. We asked her what step she could take to accomplish that goal. A year of Bible college seemed a logical next step in her thinking.

As I write this chapter, Michelle is preparing to leave in August. She took the knowledge that God had given her up to that point, and made a decision. She doesn't need to know the next step just yet. God will reveal that in His time. Since Michelle is a homebody, she still has ambivalent feelings about leaving home, but she is willing to walk through the door the Lord has opened, so that He can guide her to the next door.

❧ **Remember the godly teaching passed down to you by your parents and church leaders.** Proverbs 6:20-22 says,

> *My son, observe the commandment of your father, and do not forsake the teaching of your mother; bind them continually on your heart; tie them around your neck. When you walk about, they will guide you; when you sleep, they will watch over you; and when you awake, they will talk to you.*

At each graduation, we have left our girls with 3 John 1:4: "I have no greater joy than this, to hear of my children walking in the truth."

❧ **Choose godly friends that will steer you in the right direction.** This may be one of the most crucial tips we can offer. Friendships can either make you or break you. Since you no longer have the permanent support system of home, it is vital to establish a godly network away from home. The first year at college can be overwhelming, as you adjust to a new room, new food, a roommate, college studies, a different routine, and possible job, and car care. You need the stability that Christian friends can provide. You need at least two or three people who will direct you to the Bible for answers, who will listen and pray with you, and even cry with you when you need them to.

To Parents

Pack up, sell the house, change your name, leave no forwarding address. It's true that a sense of humor can help ease any transition. But here are some other helpful suggestions:

❧ **Grieve the loss of the past and celebrate that loss by focusing on what was good.** Reminders of your kids' growing up years will pop up at unexpected times. Prepare for times of grief. Feel the sadness. Cherish the memories. Then move on. Focus on what is left and the new life that lies ahead.

When we began this chapter, we had just put two pets to sleep within a year of each other. These pets were an integral part of our girls' childhood. As the pets grew, our girls grew. They donned party hats at birthday celebrations; jumped through hoops at a backyard circus on July 4th; thrilled the girls with four kittens born behind our water heater; rustled through wrapping paper on Christmas morn. To lose them, was to lose another living piece of our girls' childhood. It hurt because the memories were good.

Re-examine your social support network. See if you have any friends, or if you put all your eggs in the kid basket. Don't depend on your teen to meet your friendship needs. I remember feeling sorry for myself occasionally during Michelle's last year at home. Almost every evening, she had a social outing with her friends. I felt cheated and sad. One day, while she and Stephanie and I were sitting outside on our trampoline, Michelle said, "You really ought to make some friends, Mom. It would help you." I took her advice to heart, and began pursuing one or two other ladies for companionship. When I relaxed my grip on our relationship, Michelle felt more freedom to move closer to me, because she knew she was not my sole support base.

Assess yourself spiritually, emotionally, physically, mentally, and socially. Have I been using my spiritual gifts? What ways might my service to others change? What will I do with the extra time now that the kids are gone? Will I engage in volunteer work, pursue postponed goals or hobbies?

It is time to focus on your new identity, the person you are becoming. If you have fostered your own interests and talents along the way, you will not feel so bewildered when the house is suddenly empty and quiet. Working on your own individual identity, apart from your child, will ease the detachment process.

Change requires loss. There are two sides to the coin. You must lose in order to gain. No one likes to think about growth and maturity having negative aspects, but in order to grow, you must grow up and away from where you currently are. Loving detachment is exciting for both parent and child, as you both are growing in God's unique purposes for your lives.

Under the healthiest of circumstances, we will grieve this phase of our lives, but it is just that—a phase. God has many more exciting, fulfilling opportunities awaiting the couple who will reach out for God's direction and blessing.

Revitalizing Your Marriage in the Empty Nest Years

The house was deadly silent. Chuck and I looked at each other across the breakfast table. "A prelude of things to come," I muttered. He nodded, affirming my thoughts. Our oldest was living in North Carolina, our middle girl was working and preparing for college in the fall, and our youngest was out with a friend. We both felt the foreboding shadow of the empty nest years creep across the table. "I hope we're ready for this," I mused. "We will be," Chuck reassured.

Most couples share a similar anxiety when the last child leaves home. Often, the empty nest coincides with mid-life challenges and the care of aging parents, setting up the couple for multiple loss situations. Changes in routine, roles, and time, call for adjustment. In his book, *Recovering from the Losses of Life*, Norman Wright comments that, "sometimes an additional loss occurs if the couple lunges toward each other to fill the empty spaces in their lives. They may end up pushing each other away because of their intensity, and a feeling of abandonment can result."[1]

On the other hand, some couples eager to fulfill postponed goals and dreams, delve into their work or hobbies to the exclusion of their mates. Intimacy suffers. Some spouses may go looking for another person to fill that void, and thus ensues an affair. Others aren't looking, but the secretary is such a good listener that, before he realizes what is happening, an unhealthy attachment is formed. Keep your eyes and ears open at all times. Keep a healthy sense of balance in your relationship.

A marriage is vulnerable when the nest empties. With the children gone, the couple focus in on their relationship, maybe for the first time since they said, "I do." They might not like what they see. Some may choose to run. Others choose to stay in the marriage and commit to a stronger second half. The couple who has made their marriage a priority from the beginning, will discover the transition much smoother.

Nonetheless, even the best relationship needs a boost during these transition years. Try the following tips to infuse new life into your marriage:

1. Date your mate. List activities you enjoy, and number them in order of your preference. Take turns sharing your hobbies and special places of interest. Through the girls' growing years, we made it a goal to go out alone together weekly. We put it on the calendar. Otherwise, it would not have happened. Don't let other activities crowd out your couple time. You are experiencing emotions that are unique to this time. You both need this weekly refresher, for just the two of you to share feelings and enjoy each other's companionship and support.

2. Find your own outlet. With the potential to overly cling to one another as you work through this transition time, it is important to "test the waters" and find an activity that excites your soul. There is always a plea for volunteers in many wonderful community organizations, as well as at church. For Eileen, writing has given new purpose, as we make this journey from active parenting to the empty nest. For Chuck, golf has provided a much needed diversion. Remember to include some time each day giving back to others. That's the secret to true joy and fulfillment.

3. Balance time together with other pursuits. Dave Peterson, founder and president of Total Life Counseling, Inc., encourages couples to regularly evaluate their involvement in eight different areas. Consider the following as you plan out your activities on a daily basis:

- Spiritual (spending time alone with God, church work)
- Emotional (sharing feelings with my mate, outside friendships, journaling)
- Physical (recreation, exercise)
- Cultural (could be as simple as visiting an art museum, attending the symphony, or as extensive as planning an overseas trip to tour or work on a mission's project)
- Financial (setting goals for present as well as future needs)
- Marital (making time for each other, working on communication skills)
- Social (hosting parties, maintaining outside friendships, both individually, as well as a couple)
- Governmental (deciding what part you play as a Christian citizen, such as voting, lobbying, praying, making calls, writing letters)

Some of the above areas may overlap. You may decide to spend more time in one category than in another. Take your thoughts before

God and ask His input. Remember man plans, but God directs His steps. It may be helpful to make a chart on which you list each category and the time spent in each pursuit. Reassess your activities weekly, monthly, and yearly. Reevaluate. Set new goals. Share your individual plan with your mate and talk about it together.

If your life was complete before your children left home, your adjustment will be easier. If your life was never complete, you have a major task ahead. If you haven't been a healthy individual, you won't be now. This additional life challenge will only make things more difficult. You may need professional assistance as you wade through overwhelming thoughts and feelings.

On the other hand, if you have a social network in place, or extended family relationships from which you can receive empathy, support, and suggestions, you will handle this transition as a bump in the road, not a major crevice that causes you to stop your car, repair the road, then cross.

4. Keep the lines of communication open daily. Our "home-base" is at the breakfast table where we take a few minutes to read some Scripture or a Christian book, pray together, and discuss concerns. We try to manage conflicts as they arise. We deal with this issue extensively in our book, *Marriage with an Attitude*.

5. Handle anger constructively. You've heard the old adage, "Don't go to bed mad." Well, it's older than grandma. Paul preached the same message thousands of years ago when he wrote Ephesians 4:26, "Be angry, and yet do not sin; do not let the sun go down on your anger." Choose to forgive daily. Leave the past behind and move forward together.

6. Make your spouse your best friend. To be well-balanced, also include other friendships.

7. Enhance your romance. Don't get so busy with your new interests that you cheat yourself and your partner out of intimacy. You probably have more time and, perhaps, money to invest in candlelit dinners, trips, and moonlit walks than ever before. If your home is happy, you will be able to give more to others. You have more emotional energy to invest. Remember, God has an exciting path mapped out for your marriage ministry, as you recommit to serve Him together for the rest of your days.

A Word to Parents of Wayward Children

God knew from the beginning of time that His finest creation would turn against Him. How can we, as Christian parents, assume that our children will always respond positively, when Adam and Eve did not, even in an ideal setting?

When our best efforts have failed, how do we cope?

Once again commit your adult child to God. He is in control. He has His hand upon your son or daughter. God has the final word on how your child will turn out, so keep on praying and trusting Him to work even when all seems hopeless. Cling to God's promises for inner strength. And when every promise seems to evaporate like water on a hot day, cling to God Himself.

Your happiness does not depend on your child's behavior. True joy and satisfaction only come by resting in the Lord (Phil. 4:4).

Practice unconditional love in attitude and action. Only God can provide this ability, so lean hard on Him, especially if your child maligns you, disowns you, and accuses you of past parenting failures. His anger reveals his hurt and dependence upon you. Resist the urge to vent your anger on your adult child. Don't preach, ridicule, or lash out over his rebellion. It will only drive him further away. You no longer function as a parent, but as a friend, so develop a listening ear, which may just lead him back home in repentance.

Avoid blaming your spouse or any other family member for the wayward child's behavior. Distinguish between true guilt and false guilt. False guilt is when we accept responsibility for something we did not do. True guilt is when we recognize we have truly sinned. We confess that sin to God and receive His forgiveness (see 1 John 1:9).

Ask for your child's forgiveness when the Holy Spirit reveals any sin you have committed toward the child. Then, let go of the past and move on. Any true guilt will be released upon confession. But don't expect an immediate attitude change in your child. He may or may not respond, but at least you have opened a door.

Don't rush in to rescue the child from a deviant lifestyle. Back off, pray, and allow your adult child freedom to hurt enough to seek help on his own. If a parent continually moves in to help, the child remains dependent, and steps of restoration are hindered. I have dealt with incidences when a parent has tried to force an adult child into counseling. Things generally get worse. But when the parent seeks permission to share his perspective, and the adult child grants it, then the parent's suggestions are much more positively received.

Don't act out of fear. Take courage. Respect yourself and the boundaries you have set over your life and home.

Watch for signs of stress on your marriage. Keep talking and listening to one another. I remember a couple who were so fixated on their daughter's marital fiasco, that they started blaming each other. All their conversation revolved around their daughter's problems. When they realized they were driving each other away, they confessed their hurtful words, and reaffirmed their love for one another. They made a commitment to only discuss their daughter's marital problems at specific times, and conclude the discussions, planning what they could do and praying for God to meet the other needs.

Seek out a support group. Airing your feelings, hurt, anger, and pain in a safe environment can be healing. As the saying goes,

"There is strength in numbers." I lead an ongoing co-dependency support group which cycles every thirteen weeks. As people share their painful emotions and relationships with others, they experience support and empathy that bring about the healing described in James 5:16, "Confess your sins to one another, and pray for one another so that you may be healed."

By all means, nurture yourself. "Decorate your own soul" as someone once put it. Don't wait for someone else to bring you flowers, go out and pick them. Find fulfillment as you reach out to God. Ask Him to fill you and then give back to others what you have received from His gracious hand. He has a purpose in your child's rebellion, even when you cannot see how His hand is moving. Trust Him this minute with your wayward child. You placed him in God's hands once, do it again.

Chapter Thirteen

When a Spouse Leaves

> When divorce comes, we lose not only a mate,
> but... hundreds of other dreams once shared.
> ~Sue Richards and Stanley Hagemeyer~

A tow-headed six-year-old sifts through an old chest in the attic. Amidst old letters, hats, yearbooks, and a band uniform, she unearths the treasure she's been searching for—a pair of ruffled, sheer Priscilla curtains dating back to the 1940s. Her grandma had passed them down to her mother to adorn the windows of her newlywed apartment. Now, they lie buried among other castoffs of a past era.

The tiny girl quickly pulls the long curtains out of the tangled mess, slams the lid, and runs down the steps where a neighbor boy is waiting to play.

"I found it!" she exclaims, excitement mounting in her voice. She wraps the curtain around her head and shoulders while the remainder cascades behind. Grabbing a bunch of garden flowers from her mother's vase on the hall table, she singles out a rose and stuffs it in her friend's shirt pocket.

"There," she says, giving her friend a pat on the chest and stepping back to admire her prince. "Now, we're ready to get married."

"Wait a minute," the groom exclaims. "We need a preacher! We can't get married without a preacher."

The girl looks around. Spotting the dog sleeping on a mat by the front door, she says, "Corky can be our preacher! Right, Cork? Yeh, sure you can!" She takes her friend by the arm and they begin a long slow walk down the hallway.

Corky, coached by his little friends, leads the couple in an exchange of vows and the marriage ceremony is complete.

The boy runs to the kitchen, grabs an apron, and thrusts it at the little girl. "Time for lunch, dear. Fix me a hamburger, fries, shake, and for dessert—chocolate cake!" the boy orders. "Oh, and by the way, this place is a mess! Maybe you could vacuum a little." He walks to an easy chair in the living room, plunks down, and props his feet on the table.

Miffed, the girl turns and heads for the kitchen, not to cook, but to get her purse. She grabs her hat, dons over-sized heels and clops to the front door. Peering over his comic book, the boy asks, "Where are you going? And where's my lunch?"

"I'm going to have my hair done. The food is in the fridge." With that, she slams the front door and trips down the sidewalk.

Expectations Gone Amuck

We each took our turn playing bride and groom as children. What began as a childish game full of hopes and dreams of the happily ever after, led to an "I DO" at the marriage altar as adults. Before God and many witnesses, we committed our undying love and fidelity to one another. We believed our marriage would work. Then, reality set in.

Many, improperly prepared, enter marriage with underlying assumptions and motives leading to selfish actions. What we laugh about as children play is exactly what is happening in marriages today! We are a spoiled generation. Society applauds "my rights." No wonder so many well-intentioned couples end up in divorce court. We enter marriage with all kinds of expectations, some spoken, most unspoken.

Divorce or separation occurs when an expectation has been violated. Some expectations are God-given mandates as set forth in Scripture, such as keeping oneself free from adultery, or not defrauding one another (1 Cor. 7:5). We have a God-given right to expect fidelity within marriage. Other expectations are personal preferences, such as how many children to have, how to budget the money, or which in-law to visit over the holidays. In a healthy relationship, couples learn to verbalize expectations, discuss desires, and compromise.

Past and Present

When we were growing up in the 1950s and '60s, divorce was rare, especially in the Christian community. Focus was on the good of the family unit more than its individual members. Our grandparents and great grandparents, who farmed for a living, shared a common enterprise—keep the farm running, which was a day and night pursuit. They were so busy working together that they had no time or energy for extramarital affairs or idle, wandering minds. Divorce was not an option, financially. Extended family, living under one roof or close by, provided a support system. The husband saw what his wife did at home, because he worked there, too. He had a greater appreciation and dependency on her role as homemaker and caregiver for the children. They depended on each other for survival. Parting was not an option.

When the trend shifted from rural dwelling to city dwelling, and couples left the farm to go into the city, the family structure began to evolve. During World War II, women were forced into factory work because the men were at war. Women were now in the workplace in greater numbers. The trend continued to what it is today.

In a typical family, both husband and wife work, and the children are in daycare. In some cases, the wife no longer depends financially on her husband. The husband no longer draws significance as the number one breadwinner. Traditional roles are blurred. This adds more pressure, more stress, and more expectations. Roles must then be redefined to meet the couple's expectations. Each is so busy maintaining his private world of work that he has little or no respect for what the other contributes to the marriage and home. Often, couples who are married in every way except financially, find it much easier to make a split. With separate jobs and separate checkbooks, they function independently financially.

Many young couples today have more money than their grandparents did in their entire lives. They enjoy nice homes, luxury cars, and a pool in the backyard. I counseled one such couple. The stay-at-home wife had an emotional affair with a neighbor, because the husband was working extra hours to pay for the house. He wasn't there to meet her emotional needs. They had every material possession imaginable, but their marriage was a wreck. He asked her to move out of the neighborhood because of the other man, but she did not want to leave the house. He didn't trust her and she wouldn't allow trust to be built again. She kept going on walks by the other guy's house. Their boys even played together.

With the explosion of computer technology, it is interesting to observe the work trend moving back to home-based business. More and more people are leaving the rat race of the corporate world, to come home where they can once again center on family. They want to be in control of their own careers and lives. Though a new face, it's not so different from grandma and grandpa back on the farm.

The family unit influences society and vice versa. One feeds off the other. The pressures and demands placed on couples today adds significant stress on the marital relationship. Commitment to anything, over the long haul, is a dying discipline. "Easy come, easy go," is the motto.

Some enter marriage prepared to bail out if things don't work out. Others never intend to divorce, but due to diverse factors feel it is the only option. Thus, we have a society where divorce is prevalent, creating a chain reaction of losses and accompanying feelings.

Common Losses and Feelings

Multiple losses occur when a divorce takes place. A loss of companionship causes a spouse to question his identity. He wonders, *Who am I without this person?* The grief reaction is intensified if the person does not have other friendships he can draw upon. Further complications arise if a person does not find his ultimate worth and value in a personal relationship with the Lord Jesus Christ.

Some feel so insecure without their spouse that they immediately seek relief in another relationship. Often, as a counselor, I'm seeing affairs begun over the internet, either in a chat room or a dating service. Mabel tells Gertrude about the fascinating man she met over the internet. Initially, Gertrude is shocked, but the more she thinks about it, the more the idea appeals to her. Before long, Gertrude is in a chat room discussing unholy things with a strange man. God makes it clear in Psalm 1, that His child is "not to walk in the counsel of the wicked, nor stand in the path of sinners, nor sit in the seat of scoffers!" A Christian is to find his delight in God's Word and in God Himself. Focusing on the Lord during this difficult transition will provide peace and stability as the person waits for God's perfect plan to unfold.

Other life-changing losses occur for the divorcee. At least one spouse loses his home, as he must move out and seek shelter elsewhere. His contact with the children may be relegated to weekends or holidays. Social connection with existing friends may come unraveled, especially if most outings were as a couple with other couples. The Monday night bridge game at the couples' house is now moved elsewhere, since the couple is now divorced. Couple friends may actually avoid the divorced mates for fear the malady will rub off on them, or simply because they only knew how to relate to them as a couple and not as individuals.

Even church attachments can take on a new flavor—sometimes, a bitter one. One spouse has the pastor's sympathy and the other does not. I have counseled clients who attended the same church and had to switch Sunday School classes because they were no longer a couple. Because of the tension with the former mate, a divorcee often has to leave his church, thus adding to his loss. Even within the church family, a divorcee does not always find the support he needs. One lady I counseled, said she had to pay a counselor to listen because she had no other friends. No one else would listen.

Losses associated with divorce create a barrage of feelings common to other losses we have discussed. A spouse, comfortable with the marital relationship, is shocked that the other person is filing for divorce. He is thrown into a state of change that he did not ask for. He feels controlled and needlessly abused. The fact that he did not see the divorce coming, gives every indication that he did not have his finger on the pulse of the relationship to begin with.

Shock soon turns to anger, which leads to the blame game. Pointing fingers at the other mate to ease one's own responsibility in the relationship is a common defense. The spouse who walked out is angry because his partner refuses to change. His expectations in one or more areas are not fulfilled. Most likely the expectations revolve around the three biggies—sex, finances, and in-laws. Communication has broken down over the years, or was never established to begin with.

Spouses vent anger in other forms, also. Because of the broken relationship, they may be upset over new roles they must assume. One woman resented that she had to deal with household maintenance and car repairs. Her husband had always performed those tasks. One spouse was angry that he was forced out of his job and into counseling by his boss, who noticed the man's decreased productivity and insisted he get help. The man had to deal with his anger over being in counseling before he could address his divorce issues.

Feelings of anger can lead to buried resentment, if not flushed out and dealt with. Colossians 3:8 says, "But now you also, put them all aside: anger, wrath, malice, slander, and abusive speech from your mouth." Just like a musical crescendo, Colossians 3:8 presents an emotional crescendo beginning with anger and building to abusive speech. Anger initiates over an unmet, undiscussed expectation which, over time, leads to a more intense wrath, which leads to malice (evil intent). The spouse tries to get even. Slander (verbal abuse), usually behind the mate's back, follows and eventually leads to abusive speech (killing words) directed at the spouse.

Ridding your life of marital resentment is crucial for your healing. In our book, *Marriage with an Attitude,* we discuss the importance of managing anger through forgiveness:

> Managing anger is crucial. When we hold on to anger we dance like puppets on strings. And who is holding the strings? The person with whom we are angry. The steps to anger management are twofold:
>
> **1. Tell the truth in all of its pain, ugliness, and gore.** A person might say, "I'm not angry; I just haven't forgiven him." That person is in denial. Another person might say, "The Bible doesn't allow me to be angry." This refutes Ephesians 4:26 which says, "Be angry, and yet do not sin;

do not let the sun go down on your anger." This person reveals a lack of understanding of biblical teaching.

2. Choose to forgive the person. Let this process begin immediately, because it may take some time to work it through. Consider the alternative—developing ulcers, colitis, stress and gastrointestinal distress, just to name a few. Often, I receive referrals from physicians who can find no physical reason why the person is experiencing pain or distress. Later, we discover that unresolved anger is at the root. Resolving anger is one of the ways we can rejoice in the Lord and learn to be content in whatever circumstances we find ourselves (Philippians 4:4,11). In short, managing anger lets us enjoy life more. Then we are ready to stay current by not letting the sun go down on our anger (Ephesians 4:26).

Forgiving each other supports the idea that we want reconciliation, peace, and harmony rather than the prideful drive of having to be right. When we force the other person to be wrong, we both lose. Choosing to forgive is behaving God's way, as it says in Ephesians 4:31-32. We are to forgive others "even as God for Christ's sake has forgiven you." To best understand forgiveness it is important to understand what forgiveness is NOT. For example, forgiveness is not conceding and giving in to what has happened. Forgiveness is also not condoning by agreeing that what happened was okay. Forgiveness is certainly not forgetting, which is the most misunderstood concept, because people have the mistaken notion that they must forget to forgive. "Just forgive and forget," is the common saying that is imbedded in our minds. The problem is that we will never forget. In fact, the stronger the emotional impact on us, the more the memory will be deeply imprinted in our brains.

Imprinting is that process in which the brain acts like a record. When the brain receives stimuli, the information is imprinted on the brain, similar to a needle repeatedly scratching a record eventually wears a groove on the surface. The scratch widens over time and destroys larger and larger parts of the record. So it is with the imprinting process in the brain. The more the negative issue is thought about, the deeper the groove develops. To this extent, that is all the brain can think about. Each repetitive thought is a new impression.

Let's face it—our deepest hurts are thoughts we have thought about hundreds of times and the multiple impressions result in a dent the size of a canyon. This scientific phenomenon illustrates how difficult it is to forget. Also, remember that God's omniscience teaches us that He never forgets anything. So, we don't have to forget, either. In fact, we can celebrate our memories when we deal with them God's way. The remembrance celebrates how we, with God's help, conquered the hurt and pain we originally experienced. We take our pains and hurts from others and choose to forgive. This benefits us significantly by allowing us to see how God can heal even our deepest pains and hurts. Many people are helped by writing a resolution letter that details what they have forgiven and how they have forgiven. This brings closure and can be reviewed at later times of testing.[1]

When you have chosen to forgive your mate, don't bring the issue up again. Refuse to get even, thus freeing yourself and your mate from ongoing anguish. As you write your letter of resolution, include all the thoughts, feelings, and anger triggers surrounding the divorce. Identify each anger and write about it. Talk to a trusted friend, pastor, or counselor, all the while praying the Serenity Prayer: *Lord, grant me serenity to accept the things I cannot change, the courage to change the things I can, and the wisdom to know the difference.* Distinguish true guilt from false guilt. True guilt is accepting responsibility for the things you did to damage the marriage. Be honest with yourself and your mate concerning those areas. Confess those sins to the Lord and receive His forgiveness. Stop accepting responsibility for what your spouse did. Be free from the bondage of false guilt.

In addition to feelings of anger and guilt, bouts of anxiety can lead to depression if left unchecked. The person is so mentally consumed with a host of questions, such as *Why did he leave? Why now? What if my parents find out? What if he gets custody of the kids? What if I have to go to work full-time?* Because this mental energy consumes him, he lies awake at night. A variety of resulting symptoms appear, such as diminished energy, fatigue, decreased productivity, lack of concentration, feelings of hopelessness, and a change in eating patterns. Then he begins to worry that he will always be depressed. His fear leads to further anxiety. Over time, a negative spiral becomes apparent to coworkers, friends, employers, and family members. Physical symptoms may appear that lead him to a physician. Assessing that the physical complaints stem from depression, the doctor will refer the patient to a professional counselor for treatment. As the client and counselor work together to formulate a recovery plan, a support system is established.

Developing a Support Network

In order to cope with the trauma of divorce, a support base must be in place. God designed each one of us with a need for relationship. You will turn to someone. If you do not, you will turn inward and begin to shrivel as a person. You may turn to your kids for emotional support, but this will only add more stress on them.

They are already dealing with self-blame and are fragile emotionally.

In a majority of cases, extended family who are close geographically, can provide an initial buffer and help you weather the storm. Two or three trusted friends can offer a listening ear. However, be careful that the friend is not merely agreeing with you about how terrible your ex-spouse is. Nothing productive can come out of such a conversation. Look for a friend who will not only listen, but will also point you in the right direction for additional help. Most often, a divorcee needs professional guidance to unravel all the tangled issues. A good support system then, would incorporate trusted friends, family, a professional ear, and a support group, all working together to help you re-establish your life and set boundaries for yourself.

Setting Boundaries

Now that the divorce is final, it is important to establish guidelines for a new relationship with your ex-spouse. This step is important for mental and emotional stability. Since the marital union has been severed, you must not allow your ex to define and direct who you are and what you do. You must be in charge of your own feelings, attitudes, and behaviors. With the help of your counselor, you need to communicate your boundaries to your ex-spouse. One woman was having trouble with her ex repeatedly calling her on the phone, and asking her to come to his apartment to discuss remaining financial matters from the marriage. When she would arrive at his place, he would pester her to have marital relations with him. Clearly, she needed to set appropriate boundaries over their relationship. I urged her to reserve communication with her ex for the phone, and only about the financial matter.

Setting boundaries does not mean you are selfish or angry. Boundaries are a healthy way of gaining control over our own lives and fulfilling what we were created for—love. Even though the marriage is over, you can learn to love your ex as God loves you. Part of godly love is refusing to take responsibility for your spouse, thus keeping him in an immature state. With healthy boundaries you accept that you cannot change your ex; only God can do that. But you can change yourself with God's help.

Setting appropriate boundaries may be difficult for you if you never learned to communicate effectively in your marriage. That is why it is so important to have professional guidance to walk you through the healing journey. Setting boundaries is also essential to guarding your children's hearts during this rough passage.

Guarding the Hearts of Your Children

Children are usually the most wounded and most neglected victims of a divorce. They may have heard their parents arguing over them, so they assume they caused the split. Blame is so common in children that it can lead to serious depression and even suicide. Your kids will deal with this loss as they have other losses. If they talked openly about past losses, they probably will talk about this one, too.

If they don't confide in you or someone they trust, get outside help. Watch for changes in eating patterns, moods, behavior, friendships, and school performance. Some troubled kids will withdraw from society or exhibit rebellious behavior. Be alert and attentive to your children's emotional needs, even as you work through your own.

Your kids love your ex even though you may not. Don't berate your ex in front of the kids. If at all possible, encourage the kids to stay in contact with the ex-spouse.

Our prayer for you, dear one, is that you and your children will discover life after divorce as you walk down the road to recovery.

Part VI

Saying Goodbye to Youth

Live each day to the fullest. Get the most from each hour, each day, and each age of your life. Then you can look forward with confidence and back without regrets.

~S.H. Payer~

Chapter Fourteen

Growing Up and Out

> Life is God's gift to you.
> The way you live your life is your gift to God.
> Make it a fantastic one.
> ~LEO BUSCAGLIA~

Growing up from the cradle to the grave is a lifelong series of changes. At every age we say goodbye to one stage and hello to a new age.

We board the bus to kindergarten and lose the secure environs of home. Along the way we gain life experience, lose friendships, and gain others. Many watch parents separate or endure tragic illness. As life accelerates, so does the change, as we move out of the home and off on our own. We gain a job, lose a job. Make money, lose money. See one ministry opportunity open, watch another close. Hopefully, as we advance through the decades, we are not merely going through life, but growing through life. We remember our primary focus is to honor God from our youth and throughout life. Ecclesiastes 12:1 says, "Remember also your Creator in the days of your youth." Acknowledging God's authority over our lives while young provides a foundation upon which to build our lives.

The book of Proverbs, containing thirty-one chapters, offers rich practical advice for everyday living as we grow up and out of our families of origin. Reading one chapter a day, you can complete the book in a month and then begin again the next month. Keep a list of what God reveals to you in areas such as business dealings, selecting a life partner, personal habits, moral integrity, government involvement, and family relationships. You will grow stronger through the changing seasons as you apply godly wisdom to your life. We encourage you to develop the habit of studying God's Word while you are young and forming values and convictions that will influence the direction of your life.

As we approach mid-life, we experience our own aging, our parents' physical and mental decline, deal with the empty nest, and perhaps even the death of lifelong dreams. We move into retirement, either bitter or better, depending upon our attitude toward life and the way we have processed individual losses along the way. Have we grieved each loss to the point of resolution, so that there is not a domino effect? Have we claimed the Savior's sweetness over our dispositions? Do we still marvel at the wonder of life? Albert Einstein said, "There are only two ways to live your life. One is as though nothing is a miracle. The other is as though everything is a miracle."

Someone passed along this humorous sketch on the stages of life.

At age 4...	success is...	not peeing in your pants.
At age 12...	success is...	having friends.
At age 16...	success is...	having a driver's license.
At age 20...	success is...	having sex.
At age 35...	success is...	having money.
At age 50...	success is...	having money.
At age 60...	success is...	having sex.

At age 70...	success is...	having a driver's license.
At age 75...	success is...	having friends.
At age 80...	success is...	not peeing in your pants.

—Source unknown

Learning to successfully navigate the curves in the road as one advances through the seasons of life, does require a sense of humor. But it also requires a total abandonment to the purposes of God at each stage. As a child and young adult, God's plan for me was to focus on obtaining a good education, so that I could take the next step in accomplishing His purpose for me. In my twenties and thirties, God's plan for me involved rearing a family and establishing a solid ministry. Now in my forties, I feel less in control of my life than during previous periods. Even though in previous seasons I acknowledged God's control over each aspect of my life, I still felt in control. I chose the college I would attend. I chose whom I would marry. I accepted or refused a job offer. Now, with children growing up and leaving home, and aging parents with physical problems I cannot mend, I feel less in control of circumstances. I am once again obliged to reaffirm that God is, indeed, in control of every area of my life, and I am increasingly thankful that He is!

Two common experiences rise to the surface as we grow up and away from our families of origin. Along life's journey, we usually confront at least one job loss. At some juncture along the path, we may realize the death of a dream.

Job Loss

It is not unusual in our journey through life to confront a job or career change. Some contend that the average person experiences as many as fifteen job changes before retirement. Losing a job, whatever the reason, can be a devastating life event. Those whose significance is wrapped up in their work may suffer depression, lack of purpose, and loss of self esteem. A man who cannot provide for his family may feel inferior, especially as he looks around at prosperous colleagues. Forming attachments outside the office can provide a support base when and if a job loss occurs. Ultimate worth and purpose must come from a personal relationship with Jesus Christ. If we view everything we do as an expression of His power flowing through us, when a job loss happens, we will see it as an opportunity for growth. God is simply re-channeling our gifts and talents into a new endeavor. A job loss can actually be a blessing in disguise to get us out of a rut, to drive us to further dependence on God, and to teach us to use hidden or dormant gifts we never dreamed we possessed.

When a department was eliminated at the university I (Chuck) worked for, and I was told I did not need to come back to work the next day, I was in shock. I did not know how I would provide for my growing family. I questioned God's purposes and my boss's motives. I spent that evening in tears, cleaning out my office with Eileen. The next day ushered in the confusing search for other employment, which led me temporarily down one path, but ultimately down another path, allowing me to work in a facility for the profoundly mentally challenged.

This new position taught me behavior modification techniques that I use in my counseling practice today. It taught me patience, since I worked with mentally challenged adults who had little or no control over their bodily functions. I remember one woman who was self-abusive. She would literally beat herself to a pulp. As part of her program, I would walk across the floor with her, matching her steps with mine while holding her arms. Then I would put her back in her wheelchair. Exhausted, she would relax and not hit herself for a period of time.

Once, an aid was mopping up urine off the floor and a resident came over to play in the water. I told the aid I would keep the man from the bucket by redirecting his attention to another activity. Instead, the fellow dumped the bucket on me! This same guy liked to eat the mop strings. When the doctor opened him up and saw the mop in his stomach, he said, "If I hadn't seen it for myself, I wouldn't have believed it was anatomically possible." My job was to keep the man from eating anything else. He had been opened up so much, the doctor said he couldn't cut on him again. He'd simply have to pass the foreign materials! Ouch!

The job at the facility for the mentally challenged taught me things I never would have pursued on my own. It increased my humility as I learned lessons from the mentally challenged folks. My creativity emerged as I explored options to help them overcome negative behaviors. Both humility and creativity are invaluable assets for me now as I guide clients in their personal healing journey. Through that experience with the profoundly mentally challenged, I came to understand that simple pleasures, like a smile, are really the most important things in life. The job change also motivated me to complete the requirements for state licensure, and it increased my salary by two thousand dollars a year. In short, the job change proved to be an invaluable stepping stone to what I do today. It also increased my trust in God's faithfulness to provide for me and my family.

A job loss can be a chance to reassess your strengths and weaknesses. Journaling your thoughts surrounding the loss can help flush out feelings. You may then discover you can approach life with a positive attitude, which may just lead you to your next employment opportunity.

When my brother lost his job and was out of work for awhile, he used the extra time to form tighter relationships with his wife and three sons. Although it was difficult to trust the Lord through that trying episode, he made lasting memories with his family—a goal well worth the effort.

The Death of a Dream

An Olympic dream crushed. A political candidate defeated. A "D" on that research paper. The death of a dream can be as simple as resistance to one of your ideas, or as baffling as a barren womb.

Dreams keep us young, keep us reaching, growing, stretching. Our reaction to the loss of a dream depends on how much weight we placed on its fulfillment. Alexander Graham Bell said, "When one door closes, another opens, but we often look so long and so regretfully upon the closed door that we do not see the one which has opened for us." As we age, realism teaches us that we may need to adjust our dreams to our circumstances or physical condition. But we need never stop dreaming. If one dream dies and there is no way to resurrect it, then ask God for another. He is overflowing with creative options just suited to you. He wants to use you, whatever your age, to further His Kingdom.

We may need to adjust our expectations concerning a given dream. When my daughter taught me to play the guitar when I was forty-four, I did not have the agility I had at age sixteen, but I could master some skills and find joy in learning about a new instrument. I may never sing and play the guitar while leaping barefoot through the Swiss Alps, like Maria on *The Sound of Music*, but I can succeed to a certain extent.

As a counselor, deep in my heart, I want every troubled marriage, and everyone in conflict or crisis who come through my doors, to receive one hundred percent healing. As thankful as I am that most people experience positive results, not all do. My dream does not match reality. I can't let my significance be determined by the therapeutic outcome of the people I help.

After having attended a church for twelve years, we left without knowing where we would worship. This excruciating decision came from the belief that our ministry in that particular place was over. Our dream was for this church to be a body that would assimilate others into its fellowship. We labored to that end, but soon came to realize that the church was dying, because it simply was not reproducing. We had to move on. In that situation, we carried our dream with us. Even as we minister elsewhere, we still pray that God will raise up our previous church to be a mighty influence for Him in our community.

As you advance through the seasons of life with all its varied ups and downs, say goodbye to each stage. Celebrate the good memories, but move on, stepping out, and planting your foot squarely on the road that leads to your next adventure. And rejoice, for God makes no mistakes. His plan is right and good! The death of one dream merely means God is opening the way for another.

No matter how old you are, never stop dreaming. Remember Grandma Moses. An old woman, she had arthritis so bad in her hands that she gave up knitting and took up painting. You know the rest of the story.

Chapter Fifteen

Growing Down and Out

> Wife to husband sleeping on sofa:
> "Carl, if we're going to grow old together,
> you're going to have to slow up and wait for me."
> ~SOURCE UNKNOWN~

"What do you do when you are eighty-four years old and you feel like you are forty-eight?" Mom mused one day while I was visiting. Mom felt trapped in an old body. I thought to myself, *I'm forty-five and some days I feel like I'm eighty-four!*

During my devotions one morning, I came across Psalm 16:1, "Preserve me, O God, for I take refuge in Thee." Feeling challenged by some physical changes, I latched on to the first two words—PRESERVE ME! I thought, *That must be the heart-cry of every middle-aged woman experiencing graying air, failing eyesight, and bulging waistline.*

Self Preservation or Godly Preservation?

As physical appearance and performance deteriorate and mental alertness wanes, we hang on tenaciously to the last vestige of youth.

We dye our hair, exercise, take vitamins, powder, puff, flex, and beat body parts into submission—all in a crazed attempt to preserve our physical bodies from the inevitable.

While taking care of ourselves physically can boost our self-esteem and emotional well-being, I believe God's preservation runs much deeper in our lives. When we run to Him for refuge in the midst of mid-life transitions, He proves Himself a stabilizing force. He preserves our spiritual commitment to Him. He reminds us that in Him our hearts and bodies dwell securely. He will not abandon us. And though the aging process will proceed as scheduled, God promises that, "in His presence is fullness of joy and in His right hand there are pleasures forever both now and in the future" (Ps. 16:11 paraphrase).

Proverbs abounds with passages about the wisdom gained through aging. "The glory of young men is their strength, and the honor or splendor of old men is their gray hair" (Prov. 20:29), for "a gray head... is found in the way of righteousness" (Prov. 16:31). One of the benefits of living our lives by godly principles is a long life.

A deeper intimacy with God, as we mature, is the greatest blessing of growing older. We can look back over the years and reflect on how He has protected us, guided us through adversity, and laid His staying hand on every situation. Our friendship is deeper because of what He has done over the years. Our profoundest privilege is passing that blessing down to the next generation waiting to pick up the baton. Leaving a godly legacy should be our foremost passion. As Peter Marshall said, "The measure of a life, after all, is not its duration, but its donation."

> *O God, You have taught me from my youth;*
> *And I still declare Your wondrous deeds.*
> *And even when I am old and gray, O God, do not forsake me.*
> *Until I declare Your strength to this generation,*

Your power to all who are to come.
For Your righteousness, O God, reaches to the heavens,
You who have done great things:
O God, who is like You?
You, who have shown me many troubles and distresses,
Will revive me again,
And will bring me up again from the depths of the earth.
May You increase my greatness,
And turn to comfort me (Ps. 71:17-21).

Psalm 71, the prayer of an old man, is an excellent study on aging. We encourage you to read through it often as you mature.

Adjusting to the Aging Process

"You can't turn back the clock, but you can wind it up again," said Bonnie Prudden.

Indeed, our attitude toward aging will determine whether we reach out for life as a sweet gift from God or as a sour apple from Satan. We have a choice—savor the roses or whine over the thorns. Perspective is everything! It can carry us through aching backs, prolonged illness, and ungrateful offspring. One elderly lady, when asked by a child if she were young or old, replied, "My dear, I have been young a very long time" (from *P.S. I Love You*). That lady adopted a positive attitude toward long life.

I also like to encourage older folks to guard against hardening of the OUGHTERIES. It seems the older we get, the more the *"oughts"* and *"shoulds"* of life drive us to distraction, away from the current purposes of God for our lives. Every time Eileen visits her dear prayer partner, she confesses, "I hurt constantly, but God is so good!" She does not argue with God over how things *should* be. She has learned to accept the Master's plan, and adjust to failing health because she knows the Great Physician.

A few years ago, my mother declared that she was physically shrinking. This was literally true as osteoporosis had altered her bone structure. At four feet, eight inches, she could look our twelve-year-old in the eye. Now every time I come home, she seems a little closer to the floor. We joke that one day I'll come in and wonder where she is. I'll cry "Mother, Mother," and I'll look down and discover a one-inch lilliputian at my feet. Her humor over her current status helps ease my concern for her well-being. Her positive attitude eases some of the pressure in dealing with old age.

Aging necessitates decisions which require considerable adjustment. Through reading and talking with older folks, we have discovered that aging raises some thoughts, fears, and questions: *Should we sell the house and move into a retirement center or condo? Since so many memories are tied up in our homes, we grieve the loss. Should I give up driving? How many more friends must I watch die? What if I die before my mate? Who will care for him? What if I don't die before my spouse? Who will care for me? Will I remarry? Will I have the same friends? How can I serve with my failing health?* As my parents commented, "At times, we just feel 'out of it!' Cast off like an old shoe. We still have goals and aspirations, but our bodies won't cooperate. Somedays we're up, somedays we're down."

All who survive the aging process learn to rise above their circumstances and live useful lives. They learn to cope by recognizing that this phase of life will pass, just as every other phase of life has passed. One eighty-six year old said, "I've learned to keep looking ahead. There are still so many good books to read, sunsets to see, friends to visit, and old dogs to take walks with" (From *Live and Learn and Pass It On* by H. Jackson Brown, Jr.). Victorious folks accept their limitations. With failing bodies, they place more emphasis on spiritual contributions, as prayer for others, and encouraging deeds which require minimal physical effort.

Older people who live lives of excellence share some sound

advice: don't dwell in the past; do what you can do NOW! Lean heavily on the Lord for grace each day. Stay childlike—not childish—just childlike. Be flexible. Make friends of the young. Reach out to them and they will reach back. We have a gentleman in our church who is a splendid example of this. He always has an encouraging word for our young people. When his wife was alive, they opened their home for youth socials on several occasions. After her death and during a time of profound sadness, some of our young people would go and sit with him. One young man in particular would mow his lawn. This older man had given himself away and his gift had returned to him a hundred-fold.

Change your schedule occasionally. Do something spontaneous, like blowing bubbles with your grandchildren or neighbor kids. Take a walk down a different road. Get a new hair style. At eighty-eight, despite a crippling stroke, E. Stanley Jones wrote his last book, *Divine Yes,* in which he revealed one of his secrets to victorious living, "I have learned that if you are blocked on one road in life, you can always find another that will open up for you."[1]

Perhaps the two most valuable assets as we age, are a good sense of humor and an unswerving trust in our heavenly Father. When all is said and done, know what really counts.

What to Count

Don't count how many years you've spent,
Just count the good you've done;
The times you've lent a helping hand,
The friends that you have won.
Count your deeds of kindness,
The smiles, not the tears;
Count all the pleasures that you've had,
But never count the years!
—Source unknown

Part VII

Guiding Others Through the Night

Chapter Sixteen

The Church: God's Support Group

Bear one another's burdens,
and thereby fulfill the law of Christ.
~GALATIANS 6:2~

The Church needs to rise to the challenge in these critical days when shattered homes and relationships abound throughout society. The average person feels disconnected and isolated. Children are growing up without a parent, or are shuffled from one home to another.

The Church needs to be the stabilizing force in people's lives. Satan has been on a mission to destroy Christian families. He knows that if he tears down the family, he tears down the Church. The divorce rate in the Christian community is equal to that of the world. Abuse is just as prevalent in so-called Christian homes as in the world, and sometimes is administered under the guise of biblical discipline. We have only to look at our weekly prayer sheets to know how many suffer from chronic illnesses, bereavement, and job loss. More than any other agency, the Church holds the resources for healing because it knows the source of healing—the God of all comfort. So, why do we often fail so miserably at a pursuit in which we should be expert?

Complementing One Another in Our Differences

The Church has a mandate to reach out to the lost and hurting. The Body of Christ should be a hospital where the wounded can come for healing, restoration, and transformation. Christ's message was inclusive, "If anyone is thirsty, let him come to Me and drink" (John 7:37). The drug addict on the street should be welcome within our walls. The battered wife, the homeless man, those of different race and background should feel loved. As someone once said, "The ground is level at the foot of the Cross."

We believe God intends His Church to be a broad collection of folks from all backgrounds and walks of life. This is where true grace enters in as we learn from one another. As James teaches, the poor in worldly goods may be rich in faith and have a spiritual lesson for the wealthy. The under-educated may be great soul winners, while the highly educated good teachers. Reaching out to those in pain, which includes every one of us at one time or another, means understanding that we each have something different to contribute to another person's healing according to how God has gifted us. A person with the gift of helps may be most comfortable offering food and physical assistance during a crisis. Someone with the gift of mercy may offer a listening ear.

Just as God uses our differing spiritual gifts to fulfill the function of His Body, He uses our differing backgrounds to complement one another. If we are willing to adapt to one another, see things from someone else's viewpoint, and humbly submit to one another and to God, Christ's Church can do a greater work at reaching out to the lost and hurting than ever imagined. We can each respond to God's plea to bind the brokenhearted, heal the wounded, and preach deliverance to the captives.

The Church: God's Support Group

But, we must first offer our own brokenness to God, as we discussed in the last chapter. When we are on the altar looking up, we humbly submit to God's work. If He can use our pain to help us identify with another's loss, then we have discovered meaning in our hurt. We have connected with another fellow human being, just as our suffering Lord related to each one of us in His humanity.

Seizing the Moment

Those experiencing loss may be searching for meaning, security, and significance in their lives, more than when sailing smooth waters. They may be spiritually open to God. Some who are angry at God for their loss, may be more open than we think.

We each need to be sensitive to those around us: the mom at work who has a wayward son; the man next door who just lost his wife; the bed-ridden neighbor; the co-worker with the terminal illness. Listen to them. Be alert to things they say that give indication they are seeking spiritual answers. Ask them how you can pray for them. Often, unbelievers are open to the power of prayer, even if in their minds it is nothing more than a lucky charm. Their words may give you some indication of where the hurts are. If they are willing and the situation is conducive, stop and pray with the person. This is an excellent and less threatening way to get a testimony in for the Lord, than a direct confrontation with the gospel. The person will know what you believe and whom to seek out when he is ready to commit his life completely to the Lord.

God implores His Body to move out beyond the church doors—to go and compel them to come in, to visit the orphans and widows in their distress. As James says, "Pure and undefiled religion in the sight of our God and Father is this" (James 1:27). These poor souls can give us nothing of this world in return, but often they nourish our souls in spiritual ways. Joy breeds joy. Often the infirm are the most joyful. In short, we need each other for support!

Make it your goal each day to reach out to one other hurting person. Sometimes, people are aching inwardly that we do not know about. Ask God to reveal that person to you. If you are keeping the lines of communication open with God, He will place that person on your heart or bring him across your path during the day. You may not fully know the need, but God does. The joy you receive at listening to His voice and obeying is overwhelming, as later the hurting person may tell you what the hurt was.

Once I felt compelled to take a meal over to a family. The wife was pregnant and had to stay off her feet. The girls and I dropped off the meal at her home and left. Later that evening, I found a note in the door. She had been praying for God to show her His love in a special way that day, for she felt so alone. The meal and visit was just the thing she needed to lift her spirit. I, too, would have missed out on a blessing if I had not quickly responded to God's voice and done the kind deed. God is faithful to lead if we quiet our hearts and keep our minds open to His direction.

Helping Others Grieve

"Giving is the secret of a healthy life… whatever (one) has of encouragement and sympathy and understanding," said John D. Rockefeller. He had discovered what so many others have learned when mourning comes—joy comes in the giving.

Use your pain to reach out to others. Some mourners reach out in a public way, as in the case of MADD (Mothers Against Drunk Drivers). One mom's grief over a child's death at the hands of a drunk driver led her to form a national organization. You may not be inclined to reach out in a public way, but you may choose to help one other individual as God presents him to you. Use your particular spiritual gift as a ministry in that person's life.

Know that each person grieves differently. Be patient. Allow him time and freedom to work his grief out. Some days he may be

The Church: God's Support Group

"up," other days "down." He may appear to be advancing through the grieving stages and then suddenly regress. What comforts one person may cause pain for another. Some like to see pictures of a deceased loved one or make a scrapbook, while others can't emotionally tolerate the visual memory. Balance times of attention with solitude. The mourner needs time alone to process his feelings. One of my friends recently shared with me that after her husband died, she was busy for six weeks after the funeral dealing with social security issues, writing thank-you notes, and managing other practical matters. When things died down and her mother wanted to be there to help, my friend was tired and simply wanted to be alone.

Be sensitive to what the mourner needs. He does not always have the emotional energy to tell you. If you sense he wants to be alone, honor his wishes. If he wants a listening ear, be there for him.

Allow those closest to the mourner to do the bulk of comforting. When our first daughter left for college, tears poured down my cheeks. Suddenly, I felt very alone. I couldn't even speak. As our family turned to go back in the house, our second girl took me in her arms and held me. No words, just a warm hug. Exactly what I needed at that moment. It was as if the baton had been passed on to the next sibling. I felt overwhelming comfort and support in that moment. A shared common hurt can be one of the greatest steps toward healing.

Be open to tears. Remember, real men *do* cry. Jesus, man of all men, wept. When He stood at the tomb of His dear friend, Lazarus, He wept. He identified with Mary and Martha's pain and the pain of those surrounding the gravesite. He grieved a lost friendship on this earth. He was angry over the effects of sin, even though He knew that He would soon be victorious over both sin and the grave. Tears speak volumes when words cannot.

Offer a hug. Physical touch can provide healing. But ask permission first. Some are protective of their space and possessive of their grief, especially in the early stages.

Be available in the weeks and months that follow the loss. It's never too late to send a thoughtful card, in which you may share a comforting Scripture or simply remind them that you are praying. Ask the person out to lunch or go on a walk together. Offer practical help if you are able. Phone to see how he is getting along. In the case of death, send flowers or cards on anniversaries or birthdays to show you remember the deceased. The first year following a death is usually the toughest.

Listen. Many words can cause further grief. Don't try to hurry his healing or "fix" his pain. You can't. Only God can. And it takes time. Resist the urge to tell him you know how he feels. Only God understands how he really feels. A simple, "I'm sorry for your loss, I'll be praying," is sufficient. Remember Job's friends, ridiculed as lousy comforters? They did do one thing right—they came and sat with him for seven days and did not speak. How many of us would be that committed to easing someone's pain?

Talk about the deceased. Sharing memories keeps the person alive and builds a bridge with the hurting person. Most mourners want to talk about their loved ones who have died. Celebrate the memories together as we discussed in a previous chapter on dealing with death.

Don't minimize the loss with glib statements. When we miscarried, we heard well-intentioned comments like, "You're young, you can have another child." Knowing that did not ease the pain over the child we had just lost. It will help ease frustration during your own times of grief if you understand that some feel uncomfortable around grief and try to speed up the healing process. Essential to a mourner's emotional well-being is time to adequately grieve one loss before moving on to the next phase of life. Don't rush him, but don't avoid him either because you feel uncertain how to respond. Being there is enough. God will do the work of healing.

Finally, one of the best things you can do for the hurting person is pray for him and with him. Prayer unleashes God's power to work and creates a bond of fellowship unlike any other. Sometimes the grieved is simply too numb to hear our words, but a simple heartfelt prayer asking for God's grace and peace to bathe the hurting one can bring comfort. A prayer of thanksgiving for the life of the deceased can reassure the grieving one that you remember his loved one and validate his earthly existence and contribution.

Chapter Seventeen

Knowing God IS All the Difference

Faith is deliberate confidence in the character of God whose ways you may not understand at the time.
~OSWALD CHAMBERS~

We were created to know God. A deep, abiding friendship with our Creator is the best preparation for the losses of life. I like to take walks with God. I talk to Him and listen for His direction. The hurts come, but I know my soul is anchored in the Rock of Ages and my ship won't sink. When people and life disappoint me, I know I have a heavenly Father I can run to who understands and will scoop me up in His great big loving arms.

I find Psalm 16:7-11 a tremendous source of strength:

> *I will bless the Lord who has counseled me;*
> *Indeed, my mind instructs me in the night.*
> *I have set the Lord continually before me;*
> *Because He is at my right hand, I will not be shaken.*

Therefore my heart is glad and my glory rejoices;
My flesh also will dwell securely.
For You will not abandon my soul to Sheol;
Neither will You allow Your Holy One to undergo decay.
You will make known to me the path of life;
In Your presence is fullness of joy;
In Your right hand there are pleasures forever.

Meditating on these verses has carried me through many a dark night of the soul. There have been times I have awakened in the night with a crushing oppression, and I have quoted this passage over and over until God bathed my mind with His peace and lulled me back to sleep. Though the crises come, and they will, God promises to preserve me in this life as well as the life to come.

God is God. He is master over all His creation. Our times are in His hands. He orders each one of our days. And, as David says in Psalm 139:16, "And in Your book were all written the days that were ordained for me, when as yet there was not one of them." God brought us into this world and He will take us out at His discretion. His motive—first, last, and always—is LOVE! In His infinite wisdom and mercy, He spares us from deeper hurt than the immediate tragedy. He may take our loved one now to spare us from a greater grief down the road.

The call to know God is a call to suffer (see Phil. 3:10). Christ suffered to secure our redemption. If I am to truly know Him in all His surpassing greatness and glory and be filled up with a greater capacity for God's love, then I must suffer with Him (see Eph. 3:19). There is no other way. Like Jesus, I must drink the bitter cup of suffering. Philippians 1:29 says, "For to you it has been granted for Christ's sake, not only to believe in Him, but also to suffer for His sake."

I once heard Charles Stanley share a story about a man in serious pain who asked God to take it away. God said, "Okay, I'll take it away, and with it I'll take a deep understanding of My Word, a closer walk with Me, a more intimate prayer life, and a better understanding of others' pain." The man answered back, "Bring on the pain, Lord."

Our Foundation

If God is not our foundation, then He will just be another god among many. We will be carried along ruthlessly, batted back and forth by life's storms. One of our greatest gods is the god of our expectations. We didn't get what we expected out of life, so we become disillusioned, out of control, and fearful, all because we weren't willing to realign our expectations with three foundational truths:

1. **God Is.** (Heb. 11:6; Deut. 33:27)

2. **God Loves Me.** (Jer. 31:3; Ps. 136; John 3:16; Ps. 36:7)

3. **God has a good purpose for my life.** (Jer. 1:5; Ps. 139:13-17; Ps. 31:14-15)

These three realities serve as a downy cushion in the midst of life's hard knocks. When our brains say, "This hurt is wrong, this is bad," we can go back to the three foundational truths: **God is; God loves me; and God has a good purpose for my life.**

When the foundation for our lives is in place, then, over time, we can learn that God is enough to sustain us through the storm. He can navigate the ship over the rough seas, for He has mapped out its course before we were even born.

George Macdonald once said,

> We look upon God as our last and feeblest resource. We only go to Him when we have nowhere else to go. And, then, we learn that the storms of life have driven us, not upon the rocks, but into the desired haven.

Hannah Whitall Smith put it the following way in her book, *God of All Comfort*:

> No soul can be really at rest until it has given up all dependence on everything else and has been forced to depend on the Lord alone. As long as our expectation is from other things, nothing but disappointment awaits us. Feelings may change, and will change with our changing circumstances; doctrines and dogmas may be upset; Christian work may come to naught; prayers may seem to lose their fervency; promises may seem to fail; everything that we have believed in or depended upon may seem to be swept away, and only God is left, just God, the bare God, if I may be allowed the expression; simply and only God.
>
> We say sometimes, "If I could only find a promise to fit my case, I could then be at rest." But promises may be misunderstood or misapplied, and, at the moment when we are leaning all our weight upon them, they may seem utterly to fail us. But the Promiser, who is behind His promises, and is infinitely more than His promises, can never fail nor change.[1]

Yes, it is God alone who desires to come alongside us in our grief and guide us to shore. He created us, He loves us, He has an eternal plan for the good, as well as the bad and ugly rocks that line life's pathway and threaten to impede our journey. Take those rocks, build an altar, and offer yourself in worship upon it to the Lord. Focus on Him rather than the hurts. When everything else in life is stripped away, you can then discover that knowing God is all the difference.

The Greatest Loss

We have filled up many pages dealing with various loss issues. Volumes could be written on any one of these topics.

Our prayer is that in some small way we have come alongside of you as you grieve and offered a cool cup of water in our Savior's name. Directing you to God Himself is the greatest help we can offer your hurting heart. He stands with open arms ready to embrace you and guide you through the healing process.

As great as our earthly losses are, the greatest loss of all is not to know God. All other losses pale in significance. Nothing else really matters if we do not settle the question of where we will spend eternity. This earthly existence is merely a dot on an eternal continuum.

Loss originated in the garden when Adam and Eve traded in their innocence for a piece of forbidden fruit. They had perfect fellowship with God, but they sacrificed that blessing on the altar of ego. One act of disobedience set up a chain reaction of losses that rippled down through the centuries and clouds our lives and world to this day. Their loss became our loss. In order to restore us to Himself, God suffered the loss of His only begotten Son on the cross. All creation hovered to see what would happen next. Would God's principle of losing in order to gain ring true?

One more loss had to take place—a loss we each need to confront when coming face-to-face with the Savior. It is probably the most difficult loss to endure, but one that yields the greatest return. In order to receive God's gift of forgiveness, peace, and a heavenly home, we must abandon our pride, every vestige of self-righteousness, and cling tenaciously to Christ's righteousness alone as covering for all our sins. We lose ourselves in order to gain Christ. We are no longer on the throne of our lives. We recognize that we can't approach a holy God in our own goodness; there must be a perfect mediator—God's Son—who bridges the gap between us and God. When we accept that Jesus is the only way to know God (see John 14:6), then our loss of self becomes our greatest gain.

Yes, our greatest loss becomes our greatest gain. We are now in right relationship with God. God smiles and the angels rejoice. We now have the best Friend imaginable to guide us on our healing journey, for the road from loss to recovery begins and ends with God Himself! A new day dawns and we rejoice in the morning.

> *God is our refuge and strength,*
> *A very present help in trouble* (Ps. 46:1).

Notes

Chapter One: *Grief Exposed*

[1] Craig Duncan, *A Fiddling Christmas* (Pacific: Mel Bay Publishers, Inc., 1996), p. 60.

Chapter Two: *Grief Makes Me Hungry*

[1] Adapted from H. Norman Wright, *Recovering From the Losses of Life* (Grand Rapids: Fleming H. Revell, 1991), pp. 53-56 adapted.

[2] Tim Hansel, *Through the Wilderness of Loneliness* (Elgin: David C. Cook Publishing Co., 1991), p. 92.

[3] Joni Eareckson Tada and Steven Estes, *When God Weeps* (Grand Rapids: Zondervan Publishing House, 1997), p. 175.

[4] Kay Arthur, "Running for Daddy!" from *To Know Him by Name* (Sisters: Multnomah Publishers, Inc., 1995). Used by permission.

Chapter Four: *Memorial Stones to Wholeness*

[1] Hannah Whitall Smith, *God of All Comfort* (Chicago: Moody Press, 1956), p. 205.

Chapter Five: *Living With an Illness*

[1] Christin Ditchfield, "Grace for the Race," *God's World News*, September 15, 2000, p. 2.

Chapter Seven: *When Abuse Strikes: The Silent Grief*

[1] Chuck and Eileen Rife, *Marriage with an Attitude* (Tulsa: Logos to Rhema Publ., 2000), pp. 64-67.

[2] Corrie ten Boom, "I'm Still Learning to Forgive," reprinted by permission from *Guideposts Magazine* (Carmel: Guideposts Associates, Inc., 1972).

Chapter Nine: *Infertility: Empty Arms and Aching Hearts*

[1] The National Infertility Association, with Diane Aronson, Executive Director, "The Staff of Resolve," *Resolving Infertility* (New York: Harper Collins Publishers, Inc., 1999), p. 40.

[2] Albert Decker, M.D. and Suzanne Loebl, *Why Can't We Have a Baby?* (New York: The Dial Press, 1978), p. 18.

Chapter Eleven: *Losing Someone You Love*

[1] Adapted from Dr. Alan D. Wolfelt, "Helping Children Cope with Grief," from *Thanatos* (Thanatologist's Corner), Fall 1991, pp. 17-18.

[2] Hedda Bluestone Sharapan, *Talking with Young Children About Death* (Pittsburgh: Family Communications, 1979), p. 7.

Chapter Twelve: *When a Child Leaves Home*

[1] Wright, p. 148.

Chapter Thirteen: *When a Spouse Leaves*

[1] Rife, pp. 54-56.

Chapter Fifteen: *Growing Down and Out*

[1] E. Stanley Jones, excerpt from "Divine Yes," *Eternity Magazine*, February 1975.

Chapter Seventeen: *Knowing God IS All the Difference*

[1] Smith, p. 243.

Reading and Resource List

*F*or more information on natural healing, contact Hallelujah Acres, P.O. Box 10, Eidson, TN 37731 or call (423) 272-1800. Check out their Web site at: www.hacres.com.

Books:

Arp, David and Claudia. *The Second Half of Marriage.* Grand Rapids: Zondervan, 1997.

Bradshaw, John. *Homecoming: Reclaiming and Championing Your Inner Child.* New York: Bantam Books, 1990.

Bosco, Antoinette. *The Pummeled Heart, Finding Peace Through Pain.* Mystic: Twenty-Third Psalm Publishers, 1994.

Buhler, Rich. *Pain and Pretending.* Nashville: Nelson, 1988.

Carlson, Dwight, M.D. and Susan Carlson Wood. *When Life Isn't Fair.* Eugene: Harvest House, 1989.

Cloud, Dr. Henry. *Changes That Heal.* Grand Rapids: Zondervan, 1990.

Kuykendall, Carol. *Give Them Wings.* Colorodo Springs: Focus on the Family, 1998.

Lewis, C.S. *A Grief Observed.* New York: Bantam, 1961.

Martin, Dr. Grant. *Please Don't Hurt Me.* Wheaton: Victor, 1987.

Miller, Jack Silvey. *The Healing Power of Grief.* New York: Seabury, 1978.

Morrison, Jan. *A Safe Place: Beyond Sexual Abuse.* Wheaton: Shaw, 1990.

Rando, T.A. *Grief, Dying, and Death: Clinical Interventions For Caregivers.* Champagne: Research Press, 1984.

Richards, Sue Poorman and Stanley Hagemeyer. *Ministry to the Divorced.* Grand Rapids: Zondervan, 1986.

Schaefer, Dan and Christine Lyons. *How Do We Tell the Children?: A Parent's Guide to Helping Children Understand and Cope When Someone Dies.* New York: NewMarket Press, 2001.

Schiff, Harriet. *Living Through Mourning.* New York: Penguin Books, 1978.

Seamands, David A. *Healing For Damaged Emotions.* Wheaton: Victor Books, 1988.

Stern, Michael, Ph.D. and Susan Cropper, D.V.M. *Loving and Losing a Pet.* Northvale: Aronson Inc., 1998.

Stoop, Dr. David and Dr. James Masteller. *Forgiving Our Parents, Forgiving Ourselves.* Ann Arbor: Vine Books, 1991.

Westberg, Granger E. *Good Grief.* Philadelphia: Fortress Press, 1962.

Ziglar, Zig. *Confessions of a Grieving Christian.* Nashville: Nelson, 1998.

Videocassettes:

DivorceCare. Steve Grissom. Church Initiative, 1996. (Support group video and discussion series.) *info@divorcecare.org* (1-800) 489-7778.

GriefShare. Bill and Holly Dunn. Church Initiative, 1999. (Video, and discussion support group that features top experts on grief and recovery subjects.) *info@griefshare.org* (1-800) 395-5755.

Workshops:

PREP (The Prevention and Relationship Enhancement Program–addresses transitional stages of marriage.) The Center for the Family, the Graduate School of Education and Psychology at Pepperdine University. (A workshop for couples desiring to strengthen their marriage.) *info@PREPinc.com* (1-800) 366-0166.

Web sites:

Marriage Alive. 2001 <*http://www.marriagealive.com* (1-888) 690-6667.